THE PROTESTANT ETHIC
and the
SPIRIT OF PUNISHMENT

THE PROTESTANT ETHIC

and the

SPIRIT OF PUNISHMENT

T. Richard Snyder

William B. Eerdmans Publishing Company

Grand Rapids, Michigan / Cambridge, U.K.

Wm. B. Eerdmans Publishing Co.
255 Jefferson Ave. S.E., Grand Rapids, Michigan 49503 /
P.O. Box 163, Cambridge CB3 9PU U.K.

Printed in the United States of America

05 04 03 02 01   5 4 3 2 1

Library of Congress Cataloging-in-Publication Data

Snyder, T. Richard, 1936-
The Protestant ethic and the spirit of punishment / T. Richard Snyder.
p.   cm.
Includes bibliographical references.
ISBN 0-8028-4807-9 (softcover: alk. paper)
1. Grace (Theology)   2. Punishment — Religious aspects — Christianity.
3. Restorative justice — Religious aspects — Christianity.   I. Title.

BT769.S63 2001
261.8′336′0973 — dc21

00-049473

www.eerdmans.com

To Bill Webber,

whose vision and tenacity led us to Sing Sing prison

and helped keep us there,

and to the graduates of our program who opened my eyes

to a new understanding of grace

CONTENTS

| | |

PREFACE

| | | | |

I hadn't given much thought to the relationship between the tragedy of our criminal justice system and contemporary Christianity until I taught an adult education series on grace at the First Presbyterian Church in Ramsey, New Jersey. I had always been more interested in the consequences of our faith than in its orthodoxy, so it was only natural that I began by questioning how we understand grace and its implications for our world today. By this time I had been involved in New York Theological Seminary's (NYTS) teaching ministry at Sing Sing Prison — an involvement that opened my eyes to the way in which prisoners are frequently viewed as "other," as if they were a different species. But I hadn't yet drawn the connection between our theology and the way we respond to those convicted of a crime — or at least certain kinds of crime.

The next year I offered a course at NYTS looking at the possible links between certain understandings of grace and responses to crime and assigned my students to interview church members and neighbors about their views of grace. The majority, not unexpectedly, viewed grace as something extraordinary, individual, interventionist in nature, and setting its recipients apart from those who had not received it. It became increasingly probable to me that the common understanding of grace might contribute to the notion of "otherness" and the punitive spirit within our society.

Shortly thereafter I presented a paper, "The Protestant Ethic and the Spirit of Punishment," at the Annual Conference of the Society of Christian Ethics. The basic thesis of the paper was that contemporary Christianity's individualized and ahistorical notion of grace has, wittingly and unwittingly, fed the spirit of punishment prevalent in our culture. The positive feedback from my colleagues encouraged me to pursue this thesis further and to seek an alternative theological understanding that might counter the dominant mood. Historian and social ethicist Robert Craig was especially helpful in sharing resources and insights and indicating ways in which Native American cultures deal with crime. A revised form of this paper was published under the same title in *Dissent and Empowerment,* a Festschrift honoring Gayraud Wilmore.[1] Over the past few years I have tested this thesis with students at Sing Sing and at our main campus, and with adult education groups at area churches. Their insights, challenges, and endorsement of the overall direction of my work have been extraordinarily important.

In 1998 I was awarded a Faculty Research grant by the Association of Theological Schools (ATS) funded by the Lilly Endowment. This grant, combined with a sabbatical from NYTS, provided an opportunity to research a variety of restorative justice models that offer alternatives to the punitive approach so prevalent in the United States. The grant made it possible to spend time in South Africa to study both their criminal justice system and the Truth and Reconciliation Commission process, and to visit Sweden — a historically progressive society that has long practiced restorative justice. Under the guidance of Matthew Zyniewicz, ATS provided the ten grant recipients a forum in which to share our research proposals, receive critical feedback, and explore resources. Matt's support throughout the entire process was extraordinary.

I am most grateful to David Van Neel, who organized our itiner-

---

1. "The Protestant Ethic and the Spirit of Punishment," in *Dissent and Empowerment: Essays in Honor of Gayraud Wilmore,* ed. Eugene G. Turner (Louisville, KY: Witherspoon Press, 1999), pp. 16-30.

ary while in the Capetown area and who hosted and guided us throughout our entire visit, introducing us to many important individuals in the new government and to many compatriots in the anti-apartheid struggle. Many other colleagues from South Africa, including Tiniyiko Maluleke, Jim Cochrane, Russell Botman, Michael Lapsley, Charles Villa-Vicencio, and others too numerous to mention shared generously from their experience and perspectives. In Sweden, I enjoyed the gracious hospitality of Lennart Molin, president and dean of the Stockholm School of Theology, who arranged several seminars with his faculty and students. Ragnar Asserhed, Prison Chaplain Secretary for the Christian Council of Sweden, managed our itinerary throughout Sweden. Through his efforts, we were allowed inside a maximum-security prison and had extended conversations with prisoners, guards, chaplains, theologians, and former prisoners. His vast experience in and knowledge of the criminal justice system in Sweden, coupled with his deep love for those imprisoned, was a source of rich sharing. A number of persons here in the United States were extremely helpful in my research: Bill Webber, Rudy and Betty Cypser, Bob Craig, and John Humbach among them.

I also want to express my deep gratitude to New York Theological Seminary's board, staff, and faculty. In granting me a sabbatical, many persons assumed additional responsibilities. Ilene Granderson has been supportive in every way imaginable; I could not have spent the time away without her help. Barbara Austin-Lucas, Associate Dean of First Professional Programs, and Lester Ruiz, Director of the Doctor of Ministry Program, carried a heavier share of duties during my sabbatical. Various members of the faculty have been particularly encouraging as I tried to carve time out for the research and writing. We have shared conversations about aspects of the research, and Bill Webber and Lester Ruiz provided important feedback on the full manuscript.

Eerdmans Publishing Company has been an author's dream. I especially want to thank Bill Eerdmans, whose affirmation of this project grows out of a commitment to present ideas that go against the stream. He has been a strong supporter of our work at Sing Sing and a leading publisher of books dealing with justice, forgiveness, and reconciliation. David Bratt, my editor, has been encouraging, insightful, and quick to respond. I couldn't have hoped for more.

Finally, I want to thank my wife, Carole, whose continuing commitment to my work has had the profoundest impact upon me — beyond what she could ever imagine. While carrying out her own responsibilities as the executive director of a not-for-profit organization, she found the energy to encourage, prod, give feedback, and edit the entire manuscript — a gift of grace.

| | |

Getting Even: The Rush to Punish

Getting even feels good. We cheer when Clint Eastwood or Arnold Schwarzeneggar gives the enemy what they deserve. Even though movies such as *Pulp Fiction* or *Apocalypse Now* raise uncomfortable questions about the cost of violence, for the most part we find satisfaction in vengeance. We'd rather turn the knife than turn the other cheek.

Nowhere is this spirit more evident than in our rage to punish those who commit crimes. That's what prison is all about. Most of us want those who have done wrong to be punished — not healed, but punished. And so we have created a penal system that mirrors our urge to punish. But what we have created to address our need for vengeance reveals a cancer within the national culture that has the potential to destroy us.

I didn't always think this way. Like many in our society, I was raised to think that no evil deed should go unpunished, that criminals deserve what they get, and that the responsibility of the "good guys" is to stamp out or cast out the "bad guys." Growing up during World War II made the lines between good and evil seem glaringly clear. Neither I nor most of those whom I knew harbored any doubts about our calling to rid the world of the demonic forces of hatred threatening the civilized world. And so it was no great leap to come to the same conclusion with respect to those who commit crime. The worse the deed, the greater the punishment. Once killed or put away, "they" were no longer of concern to me. "They" deserved what they got and I could go on with my life.

This perspective on life gradually changed as I became aware of the complexity of evil and of the frequent complicity of presumed "good guys" in the dynamics of evil. Studies in history opened my eyes to the steps taken by the United States and others to contribute to the seeds of World War II, the Korean War, and the Vietnam War. But somehow a similar realization about our criminal justice system came more slowly.

Though I knew about police corruption, the FBI's infamous reputation, and the occasional death row prisoner who was found to be innocent, the criminal justice system rarely entered my mind. The walls that confined the imprisoned served to shut them off from my line of vision. Out of sight, out of mind. My myopia was shattered when Bill Webber, then the President of New York Theological Seminary, initiated a Master of Professional Studies program inside the walls of Sing Sing prison in 1983. Although I was part of the decision to begin the program, the full impact of what we had begun did not fully dawn on me until the following year, when I taught a semester-long course titled Introduction to Ethics with fourteen men in the second entering class. Since then, as professor and academic dean, I have had the opportunity to teach, correspond, and meet with classes, individual prisoners, and graduates who have been released. During that time I have been forced to recognize the punitive nature of our penal system and its devastating consequences for the prisoners as well as the larger society.

Everywhere we turn, people are getting even. While Yahweh may have said, "Vengeance is mine, I will repay," it would seem that our society either considers itself to be God or has concluded that God's promise is vacuous. Nowhere is this spirit of punishment more visible and more virulent than in our prisons. Dostoyevsky wrote that the soul of a society can be measured by its prisons. What we do to those we incarcerate suggests that our soul is cold to the point of death.

Like most who come to a passionate awareness of a particular injustice or problem, I assumed that others would see the light and be moved to seek a solution. But despite the Attica uprising, despite books and movies such as "Dead Man Walking" and "Shawshank Redemption," despite the increased exposure in the media of the tragic consequences of our present criminal justice system — its failure to rehabilitate, extraordinary expense, racism, brutality, and frequent mistaken convictions — society seems more intent than ever on exacting vengeance upon those convicted. In the fifteen years since I first became aware of the problems of our penal system, matters have gone from bad to worse.

Perhaps, I thought, the problem is that we lack more humane alternatives. If we had something better to put in place of the current system, maybe people would support reforms. But my research has uncovered myriads of alternatives that have been around for centuries — alternatives that are more rehabilitative, more humane, and more beneficial to the victims, perpetrators, and the larger society. The basic problem, I have come to conclude, is neither a lack of awareness nor a lack of alternatives but rather that our culture is captive to a spirit of punishment. Until we address this spirit, all calls to reform will fall upon ears that cannot hear and hearts that cannot feel.

Since 1983 I have been teaching at Sing Sing, where each year between fourteen and sixteen men are selected from among fifty or sixty applicants throughout the New York State Correctional System. Some are already incarcerated at Sing Sing, while others are transferred from other state prisons. You might expect that after fifteen years one would become accustomed to the place, but I have not. Each time I go through the gate check — removing everything from my pockets, taking off my belt and shoes, walking through the metal detector, having my briefcase searched — I become uneasy. It is only the beginning of a long trek through a series of eleven locked gates and scrutiny by innumerable guards. Each gate closes behind me with a heavy thud. Through the windows I glimpse vistas of the Hudson River, meandering idyllically along its circuitous path cut through the hills that border it. The scene is marred only by the bars on the windows and the rolls of razor wire that top the walls surrounding the prison.

When my escort deposits me in front of the guard station inside the chapel and I sign in yet again, I am finally on my own. Making my way down the steps at the back of the chapel I enter a small room crowded with the fifteen or so students in their drab green fatigues or other approved prison garb. They've saved a seat for me, carefully positioning themselves in territorial formation that has meaning only for them.

Despite the bars on the windows and the razor wire visible through them, my angst disappears in the classroom. The incredible enthusiasm for learning, for sharing, for wrestling with ideas, for growth, and for change has transformed the dynamics of my temporarily circumscribed world. Gathered here are men convicted of such felonies as murder, armed robbery, drug possession, drug dealing, and a host of other crimes. Some are innocent, the victims of frame-ups and plea-bargaining. Many are guilty and admit to it.

Most are already significantly different from the persons they were when they were admitted. Many have had conversion experiences, recovered forgotten roots, developed job skills, furthered their formal education, reconnected with families, and mastered personal discipline. While a few were well educated and privileged before they were convicted and imprisoned, most of the men have earned their high school GED and/or their bachelor's degree while behind bars. Some of them are fully capable of Ph.D. studies. A sense of purpose fills the room. Questions fly. Challenges of one another and the professor come frequently and vigorously.

In the midst of this exciting educational exchange, a guard comes in to take a head count. A sullen silence comes over the room while ID's are collected and each prisoner's number is noted. Then, as silently as he came, the guard departs. No words have been exchanged, but the communication is as dense as a thick fog. Moments before, these men have been vitally engaged in profound exchange and struggle with truth and each other. Now they are once again reduced to numbers.

They recover quickly, and soon after the guard has left, the pace and intensity of the dialogue return. When I leave, I feel exhilarated by the exchange that has occurred. It never fails. It is among the most exciting teaching I have been privileged to experience. I am amazed at the depth of their faith, the keenness of their minds, and the angle of their perspective. I love going there.

Departing from the prison I retrace the same steps I took earlier in the day, with the exception of the search. My escort, a guard for more than eleven years, echoes words I have heard frequently from other guards. "Why do you waste your time coming here? These guys are scum. You can't trust any of them. They're all con men. They should just lock them up and throw away the key. The only thing they understand is force." By the time I make it back through the last gate the oppressiveness of Sing Sing has once again claimed me. I am relieved to be out, to be going home. I hate going there.

These few hours that we have shared are an oasis in the midst of a hellish place of punishment. The depression I feel as I leave is a reflection of the oppressive reality in which the prisoners must remain. I have visited them in their cellblocks, in their recreation areas, in their hospital rooms. A spirit of punishment permeates the prison; it cannot be escaped. There are oases, such as our program and others, but for the majority prison is only a desert, a wilderness of punishment. That there is guilt involved is often uncontested; many of the men admit their guilt and recognize the necessity for making things right. Incarceration could be a time of regeneration, rebirth, renewal, rehabilitation. That might be a useful, worthwhile reason to be there. But that is not why they are there. They are there to be punished.

There is a spirit of punishment in the air. Our society is wallowing in the ethos of punishment, nowhere more evident than the way in which we deal with criminals, but not limited to that response. There is a widespread vitriolic response to people who are different, whether because of color, sexual orientation, abilities, language, country of origin, or physical condition. The 1993 movie *Falling Down* depicted the depth and scope of the rage. A middle-class white man (played by Michael Douglas) victimized by downsizing finally loses his balance in one of Los Angeles' notorious traffic jams. Most of us can identify with his rage up to that point. But in an orgy of vengeance that follows, he turns against everyone who is different from him, starting with an Asian shopkeeper, then Latinos, blacks, and women. All he wants to do is to get even for the losses in his life. Former president Reagan reinforced that spirit with his bullying arrogance, "Make my day." The murders on our Texas highways are a symbol of a nation that is increasingly quick to punish those we judge to be offensive or bothersome. Schoolmates are shot for their rejections. Cries raised by talk show hatemongers for tougher sentences are cheered by the masses. President Bush's infamous Willie Horton election advertisements fed upon people's fears and the hunger for increased punishment. Governor Pataki followed the lead of many other governors in calling for an end to parole for persons convicted of violent felonies, regardless of the personal transformation that may occur during their imprisonment. A spirit of punishment runs rampant in our society.

Former New York State governor Nelson Rockefeller has had his name affixed to a mandatory sentencing law, which he led the fight to pass. The Rockefeller Law makes it mandatory for those possessing four ounces of an illegal drug (or two ounces with an intent to sell) to be sentenced to prison for a minimum of fifteen years for a first offense and a minimum of twenty-five years for a repeat offense. This mandatory sentencing is still in effect, contributing significantly to the overcrowding of New York's prisons.

Mandatory sentencing, for which there can be no mitigating circumstances, is rooted in a "get tough, punish the offender" mentality. It has caused enormous damage. One of its most devastating consequences has been on the many poor women from Third World countries who have been either forced (at threat of their lives or their children's lives) or duped into becoming couriers of drugs. Often referred to as "drug mules," these women have been the targets of inordinate and insensitive punishment automatically meted out to them. Even when it is clear that they were forced into such actions, the judge has no alternative but to enforce the sentence.

In 1994 the federal government approved the Omnibus Crime Bill, allocating billions of dollars for new prison construction and 100,000 more police officers. Now children can be tried as adults for many federal crimes, membership in a street gang is a federal offense, forty-seven crimes are punishable by death, and persons who are convicted of a third felony (even a low-level felony) are automatically sentenced to life. An editorial in *The Nation* said of the Senate's version, "The Senate's vindictive spirit is captured by the 'three strikes you're out' amendment, approved 91 to 1 . . . anyone convicted of a third felony would automatically receive life in prison without parole, regardless of the offenses."[1] Many states have followed this federal example.

Not surprisingly, the number of persons imprisoned has continued to rise. Double and triple bunking is becoming more prevalent. One prisoner wrote of his experience of being placed in double bunking following an unsuccessful appeal to the parole board:

> I am a nonsmoker with a medically documented history of respiratory problems. . . . I have now been in double bunking status for two weeks, yet in all that time, I have spoken to the other guy in here with me not more than 20 minutes combined! . . . the other guy is a heavy chain smoker . . . my lungs are giving me serious chest pains.
>
> This double bunking is the most inhumane, humiliating, degrading, stressful, and unsanitary condition that I have ever been exposed to through my 25 years of incarceration. . . . I cleaned particles of feces (not mine) from inside the toilet with my hand wrapped only in toilet tissues (there is no toilet brush). . . . I turned my head one night and witnessed the other guy in the cell with me masturbating, only two feet away. I've smelled a thousand farts and smoked at least a thousand cigarettes of second hand smoke.
>
> The sink is only one inch from my bed, which constantly

1. *The Nation*, Dec. 6, 1993, p. 677.

sprays water on the bed. The toilet is only 17 inches from my bed. . . . The space between my bottom bunk and top bunk is only 32½ inches, which prevents me from being able to sit up in the bed. . . . I can't last much longer under these conditions.

With the rise in the number of prisoners has come an attendant rise in prison construction. It has become a boom industry. Nationwide, the number of beds in state and federal penitentiaries increased 43% from 1990 to 1995, according to one Justice Department survey.[2] Although the crime rate has dropped every year for the last eight years, the number of prisoners has increased. The Justice Department reported that in 1990 there were 1.1 million persons incarcerated in state and federal prisons. By 1997 that number had reached 1,725,842.[3] Today that number approaches 2 million. Recent legislation has intensified the building craze. Prison construction and its related expenditures are now among the top two or three largest budget items in many states. With such an enormous investment in prisons, social investments in such areas as education, health care, children's services, affordable housing, and other basic human needs have been significantly reduced.

Perhaps the most wrenching consequence is the lowering of the age at which persons can be sent to prison. In 1996, Judge Carol Kelly of Cook County, Illinois, sentenced a twelve-year-old boy to a state juvenile penitentiary, making him the nation's youngest inmate at a high-security prison. The law, which made his sentencing possible, permits children as young as ten years of age to be sent to either medium- or maximum-security prisons.[4]

Another consequence of our new national legislation is an expansion of the list of crimes that can bring the death penalty. For many years capital punishment was considered unconstitutional, but in 1976 the Supreme Court ruled it permissible under certain circum-

2. *New York Times,* Nov. 2, 1997.
3. *New York Times,* August 9, 1998.
4. *New York Times,* Jan. 30, 1996.

stances. As a result of this ruling and the new guidelines, thirty-eight states now approve the death penalty and over three thousand persons now await execution on death row. The return and increase of capital punishment have been welcomed by many of our citizens. Reminiscent of the bloodthirsty crowds at the ancient gladiatorial arenas, advocates of capital punishment gather outside the prisons to celebrate with parades, flags, banners, music, cheering, and fireworks as the hour of execution strikes.

What lies behind this increasing call for punishment? Human existence is complex and our behavior is shaped by many factors. Genetics, environment, nurture, and will all have a bearing upon our identity and behavior, so it is difficult to assign causal connections. Indeed, it would be foolhardy to suggest a single cause, as some have tried to do. Perhaps the most realistic approach would be to assemble something on the order of a collage.

One factor that has fanned the flames of the punitive spirit may well be the sheer increase in the amount of crime within this century. Lawrence Friedman, in his book *Crime and Punishment in American History,* cites some startling statistics:

> In 1990, 2.3 million Americans were victims of "violent crime," according to figures compiled by the Bureau of Justice Statistics. . . . The total number of crimes, including thefts, was something on the order of 34.8 million.[5]

Even though the number of crimes has been decreasing during the past seven or eight years, the total number remains staggering, and the likelihood is that most of us either have been a victim or know someone who has been a victim. The normal response to the experience of being criminally victimized is fear, anger, and a desire to get even. We want to stop the crime by any means necessary, and we assume that punishment will serve as a deterrent.

5. Lawrence M. Friedman, *Crime and Punishment in American History* (New York: Basic Books, 1993), p. 451.

Many consider the media to be the greatest influence on this rising spirit of punishment. While there is debate about drawing a direct correlation between the media and human behavior (e.g., the debate about the impact of media upon violence, abuse of women, use of cigarettes by young people, etc.), it is my contention that contemporary electronic and visual media have fostered significantly the spirit of punishment. How many times can we see the Indians portrayed as brutal savages deserving of death before we begin to cheer for the cowboys? How many violent police stories do we have to watch before we find ourselves eerily exhilarated by the violence meted out to the "bad guys"? How much saturation by cartoons do we need before we think that "wasting" our enemies is "cute"?

The media use crime to capture the public's attention. News is sensationalized, and nothing is perceived as more sensational than crime, so it captures our front pages and devours the lead space in radio and television news programs. Despite the drop in crime over the last six years, it continues to occupy the headlines. In addition to sensationalizing news through an obsession with crime, the media routinely and predominantly portray people of color as the perpetrators, reinforcing the deep racism of our nation. This makes it easier to embrace punishment, because the criminals are different from the majority. Never mind that whites commit more crime than blacks; the myth prevails.

John Humbach, a professor at Pace University School of Law, suggests that retribution is a "natural" human desire growing out of the evolutionary process and the will to survive.

> . . . human beings evolved the retributive urge, the innate feeling that offenders deserve pay-back, as a part of the human behavioral repertoire in order to meet the survival needs of an earlier time. . . . An "appetite" for retribution was something that individuals living in social groups simply had to have in order to hold their own against the constant possibilities of encroachment by other members of the group and by other groups. Accordingly, such an appetite would have evolved among those

who succeeded in leaving their genes in subsequent generations
. . . becoming our ancestors.[6]

Each of these is a plausible explanation for the rise of a spirit of
punishment in the land; taken together, they provide fertile avenues
for further exploration and action. But the role of Christianity in fan-
ning the flames of punishment also warrants investigation. I propose
that there is a connection between the punitive ethos in our society
and Christian theology as it is popularly understood. I am interested
in the ways in which the theology by which we live has wittingly or
unwittingly played into the hands of such a spirit — in what ways, if
any, the heritage of a largely Protestant ethic and theology gives rise
to or provides support for the spirit of punishment.

There is often a gap between what we actually believe and what
we think we should believe, between official and operative theologies. Official theology is the theology created by our particular orthodoxy, while operative theology consists of the beliefs that inform our
day-to-day lives. This distinction is rather like the difference between the commonly cherished belief in the importance of "till death
us do part," and the commonly practiced "till divorce do us part."

It is my thesis that the dominant understanding of nature and
grace within popular religion today, especially in its more Protestant
form, makes room for and sometimes even gives rise to a spirit of
punishment. I begin by examining the dominant Protestant notion of
grace and its limitations. It is precisely at the point of the limitations
that this theological understanding plays — often unwittingly — into
the hands of a society that clamors to punish. These limitations are
not necessary to Christianity, nor are they necessarily faithful to its
earliest roots. But a distortion of the understanding of grace feeds
into a punitive culture that builds upon and is reinforced by the distortion.

Two crucial distortions prevail. The first is an absence of creation

6. John Humbach, "Blame, Retribution and the Problem of Criminality" (un-
published paper, Sept. 27, 1997), p. 37.

grace. Because of the strong emphasis upon the fall, original sin, and total depravity, it is difficult to find within Protestantism an affirmation of the beauty, goodness, and worth in all creation. Whatever grace creation once possessed has been lost with the fall. Only in redemption is grace restored. That being the case, it becomes easy to think that those whose condition is less than favorable (such as criminals, the sick, the poor) are reaping the just deserts of their unredeemed state. It is then but a short step to dismissing them as less than fully human.

Historically, many people have assumed that there is a connection between deviance from the norm and unregeneracy. The New Testament Scriptures are filled with stories of persons whose sick or impoverished condition was assumed to be the result of their sins — or the sins of their forbearers. Those who were not in such unfavorable conditions considered themselves to be superior and worthy to be judges of the outcasts. This attitude is epitomized in the self-righteous prayer, "God, I thank you that I am not like other people: thieves, rogues, adulterers or even like this tax collector" (Luke 18:11). This same attitude toward certain people as "other" is fostered by contemporary Protestantism as it rejects or overlooks the reality of the grace that is present in all of creation. When one focuses on "deviance," in whatever form, it is easy to forget one's own frailties as well as the beauty, dignity, and worth of the other.

The second distortion of most Protestant theologies of grace is that in the process of redemption grace is understood almost exclusively in individualistic, internalized, non-historical terms. The social-historical dimensions of grace that are necessary for holistic redemption are ignored.

It would seem inconceivable to most North American Christians that redemption is as much a corporate and institutional dynamic as it is a personal one. When we miss this truth, it is easy to fall into the trap of assuming that the sole focus of redemption should be upon the person who has fallen. But such a limitation flies in the face of the reality of God's love for all creation. It is not only persons that need redeeming; it is also public policies, institutions, and the corporate structures of our lives. The contemporary penal response to crime represents an individualized notion of redemption.

I do not mean to advocate a simplistic connection between certain ways of thinking about grace and punishing forms of behavior. It is important to note that these ways of thinking about grace contribute to such behaviors primarily because there is a larger hegemony within which they come into play. As Max Weber showed in *The Protestant Ethic and the Spirit of Capitalism,* the Calvinist understanding of vocation did not, in and of itself, produce capitalism, but it did play into capitalism's hands. According to Weber, Protestant theology fit with the flow of a developing capitalist culture, contributing an ethic that provided further support to and an extension of a spirit already at work. Similarly, the theology of grace that I have sketched comes into play within an already given cultural context, within an existing hegemony that, over the years, it has helped to create and support. It is a hegemony that divides people between "them" and "us," the singularly most virulent form of which has been racism. When individualized grace is linked with a culture of racism or any other kind of superior/inferior ontology, a spirit of punishment is inevitable.

This does not imply that the spirit of punishment exists only in a racist culture or only in direct correlation with racism. There have been many other objects of the rage to punish: the response of Salem to its "witches," the treatment of workers by management and owners during the late nineteenth and early twentieth centuries as they sought to organize unions, or the persecution of homosexuals in many societies down through the ages. The urge for punishment clearly does not need racism in order to thrive, but it helps.

We see the spirit of punishment at work in its starkest form today within our criminal justice system. One cannot help but wonder what role racism plays, since a grossly disproportionate number of those incarcerated and punished are people of color. In 1995 the *New York Times* reported that nationally, "one in three black men in their 20's is imprisoned, on probation or on parole."[7] And Hispanics are

7. *New York Times,* Oct. 8, 1995.

the fastest growing population within our prisons. American society, while less overtly racist than previous times in such matters as fair housing and public accommodations, nonetheless largely continues to think of and treat people of color as inferior. The tenacity of contemporary racism has been well documented by Ellis Cose[8] and Cornel West.[9] One has to wonder if there isn't a connection between building more prisons, demands for harsher sentences and prison conditions, the call for capital punishment, the mood to deny pardon and parole, and the fact that the majority of our prisoners are persons of color. One has to wonder if our penal response would be so punitive if more convicted criminals were middle-class and white.

If we believe that all persons are essentially corrupt save for the extraordinary intervention of God's grace in their lives, it is a simple step to think that those who are poor, or sick, or in trouble with the law, or different from us in any way are somehow evil. The redeemed are God's children; the unrepentant are children of Satan. The demonization of those who are different or who challenge the status quo seems almost ingrained in human nature, and it has gone largely unchecked in Western culture. The step from the recognition of difference to the assumption of superiority and inferiority, which is the root of racism, is a simple one. This connection may not always be a conscious one, but it is pervasive.

Even for those who do not consciously think in these terms, the traces of belief in purely individualized grace are present. "There but for the grace of God go I" can be heard on the lips of even the most secular person. Such a phrase may connote humility, but it often thinly masks smugness and an underlying sense of superiority.

As we know, racism, especially in its post-plantation, neo-colonial form, can be very subtle. So too can be the factors that support or extend it, including religious teachings and biblical interpretations. It is often difficult to discern the connections, but in this case I am convinced of a clear link between some biblical interpretations

---

8. Ellis Cose, *The Rage of a Privileged Class* (New York: HarperCollins, 1993).
9. Cornel West, *Race Matters* (New York: Vantage Books, 1995).

and racism. Furthermore, I believe that the popular notion of individualized grace, when set in a context of a racist culture, significantly contributes to the spirit of punishment.

This claim, of course, demands fuller substantiation and development. If I am correct that the spirit of punishment in our society today is fed by and related to a basic Christian (largely Protestant) misunderstanding of grace, then it is incumbent upon us to discover other ways of thinking about God and God's grace that might provide a foundation for a more humane response to crime or deviance from the norm. Such suggestions may only be partial, but perhaps they can contribute to the larger dialogue among those who wish to see a more humane world. I find clues for another understanding of humanity and God in some of the alternative responses to crime that have been broadly categorized under the term "restorative justice." Throughout history and throughout our world today, there are alternatives that treat persons who commit crimes as part of the community, and hence that seek to restore them to a healthy place in the community. These alternatives do not focus on the perpetrator alone but also upon the victims and, most fundamentally, upon the community. While not utilizing the concept of grace as an operational understanding, they nonetheless reveal an approach to all persons as graced, no matter what their actions may have been. That is, they affirm the dignity, worth, and beauty of all persons, and seek to restore them to their wholeness. At the same time, these alternatives avoid the individualistic fallacy, as they understand that it is not only the perpetrators who must be restored, but also the fabric of the society that has been unraveled by their actions.

In using these alternatives as clues to the future, I intend to explore their philosophical and spiritual foundations. This leads to an examination of some foundations for restorative justice within the Judeo-Christian tradition, in particular the notions of covenant, incarnation, and trinity, which offer us ways of understanding the essential connectedness of all of creation and hence its essential dignity and worth. While these doctrines historically have not been seen as having a direct connection with issues of criminal justice, I find that they present enormous implications for challenging the spirit of punishment in our world today.

Finally, such a rethinking of theological foundations for criminal justice leads us to new ways of thinking about transformation, both personal and systemic. We must broaden considerably our notions of what constitutes evangelism, the spreading of the good news. Largely, it has suffered the limits of redemptive grace: individualistic, internalized, and ahistorical. True conversion must involve every level of life, from attitudes to public policies, from persons to institutions. Just as our response to crime unveils the prevalence of punishment, so too it has the potential to unveil the fullness of the redemption that we have to proclaim.

| | | |

CHAPTER ONE

The Air We Breathe:
Hegemony and the Spirit of an Age

Nearly everyone sings it, it seems. "Amazing Grace, how sweet the sound, that saved a wretch like me. I once was lost, but now am found, was blind, but now I see." And not just in church. My wife Carole and I spent one Christmas Eve on an overnight train to Florida. After all the carols had been sung, one of the passengers requested "Amazing Grace." Almost everyone joined in the singing, Christians, Jews, and the non-religious — even those who might reject the theology of the lyrics seemed to know it. It is part of the culture. Recently, I heard it played between innings at a professional baseball game.

As the advertisement says, "you don't have to be Jewish to like Levy's Jewish Rye bread"; in the same way, you don't have to be Christian to sing "Amazing Grace." It has become a popular song, part of the culture, regardless of its origin and regardless of the particular interpretations of its meaning within the walls of the church. And herein lies an important truth. A popularized form of Christian theology, especially in its Protestant form, has also become part of the air we breathe.

Throughout history the contours of the culture have been shaped by the religion or religions present within it. The obverse is also true: religion has been shaped by the culture around it. At times the religious elements are obviously and consciously part of the larger culture, as is the case with the inscription on our currency, "In God We Trust," or the emperor Constantine's use of the cross in battle. Much of the time, however, the influence is considerably more subtle.

Mechanisms of Oppression: Force, Ideology, and Inspiriting

The Christian church has been engaged with the culture in both overt and covert ways, intentionally and unintentionally, since its inception. H. Richard Niebuhr's classic study *Christ and Culture*[1] documents some of the forms this engagement has taken, from endorsement to rejection to attempts at transformation. He does not, however, undertake an analysis of the mechanisms of that engagement. Generally speaking, there are three broad ways in which the church has been related to the larger society, through force, through overt ideology, and through the more diffuse and covert process of shaping the spirit of the times. Even those responses of withdrawal from the culture have had their inspiriting impact upon it. We can see each of these three mechanisms at work in the church's history.

Force has often been an instrument of engagement on the part of the church. Seeking to shape the culture to its will, the church has turned to the sword, burning at the stake, imposing laws and sanctions, political manipulation, social ostracizing, and physical banishment. Some of the more infamous instances of the use of force such as the Crusades, the Inquisition, the Puritan Revolution in England, and the Salem witch trials are familiar to any student of history. At the foundation of the Reformed Protestant heritage lies one of the most explicit uses of force by the church to shape society, Calvin's theocratic experiment in Geneva. Making use of laws and public policy, Calvin sought to create a society answerable to the sovereign

---

1. H. Richard Niebuhr, *Christ and Culture* (New York: Harper and Row, 1951).

God. To do so he and other city leaders resorted to dramatic steps in law enforcement, including burning Servetus at the stake as a heretic. In each of these cases the church was not simply a motivator, justifier, or supporter of change; rather, it was the overt and chief instrument of the action itself.

More often the church has served as the supporter of others' force, using its teachings or allowing them to be used as ideological justification for some public action and policies. Luther's letter to the German princes provided rationalization for the violent suppression of the peasants' rebellions. Within our own nation, the idea of Manifest Destiny served as a justification for and defender of public policy. Manifest Destiny portrayed the United States as the new Israel, the chosen people, with a mandate from God to bring our way of life to the benighted heathens living in darkness. This theology provided an overt ideology for United States policies of expansionism and domination during the late 19th and early 20th century.

The fight for "true" and "pure" ideas continues today on a variety of fronts, with the church providing ideological support in the struggle for and against communism, homosexual orientation, and evolution, to name just a few. Each of these struggles is far more than a simple religious issue, having to do with economic or political control. But in each of these controversies the church and its doctrines have been used to justify given positions.

Both the direct use of force by the church and the ideological role of religion are overt, readily observable, and quite intentional. However, not all religious influence is so obvious or so intended. Sometimes religious beliefs, attitudes, values, conceptions, and orientations become part of the air we breathe, a silent or hidden part of the culture, the result of certain religious beliefs being taken for granted. There are some things that never have to be mentioned because they are so commonplace that they move to the level of unspoken assumption.

Such, for example, is the case with the modern scientific mindset. At its foundation lies the fundamental assumption of the human capacity and prerogative to experiment with, control, and even exploit nature. This basic assumption was seldom questioned during the heyday of modernity. It has been an unexamined Western cultural presupposition, though one not shared by many non-Western or traditional cultures. Only as the destructive and potentially life-threatening consequences of this stance have become evident has public debate around this "common sense" belief surfaced.

Much of this debate has focused on the subtle but pervasive influence of a theology of a hierarchy of being, goodness, and worth, in which humans are thought to stand above nature, controlling it. As Thomas Berry points out, modern theology (from Descartes onward) has failed to understand the enchantment of nature — the fact that the earth is a "numinous" community. Our failure to recognize this is responsible for the current ecological disaster.[2] Sallie McFague speaks of the Christian influence in terms of a monarchical metaphor for God that ". . . attends only to the human dimension of the world; and it supports attitudes of either domination of the world or passivity toward it."[3] These presuppositions have functioned at a covert level of assumption and become part of the spirit of the age, and thereby a critical aspect in the dominant hegemony.

Both force and ideology, when used as mechanisms of control, demand self-consciousness on the part of their wielders, but the third mechanism of social influence, what I call inspiriting, is much more subtle and often less consciously or even unconsciously used. Cornel West offers us insight into this dimension of social control and influence in his interpretation of Antonio Gramsci's notion of hegemony. West defines hegemony as "the set of formal ideas and beliefs and informal modes of behavior, habits, manners, sensibilities, and outlooks that support and sanction the existing order."[4] While Gramsci included formal ideas and beliefs in his understanding of what constitutes hegemony, I find it useful to label the more directly

2. Thomas Berry, *The Dream of the Earth* (San Francisco: Sierra Club Books, 1988), esp. Chapters 1-2.

3. Sallie McFague, *Models of God* (Philadelphia: Fortress Press, 1987), p. 69.

4. Cornel West, *Prophesy Deliverance* (Philadelphia: Westminster Press, 1982), p. 119.

formal conceptualizations as ideology and the more indirect and informal beliefs, habits, everyday behaviors, sensitivities, aesthetic appreciations, and perceptions as broadly cultural, as constituting the air we breathe. Admittedly, such a distinction cannot finally be held to, for it is clear that overt ideological claims are, in a very real way, part of the air we breathe. They shape public life, aid in the formation of perception, and underscore what we value. The metaphor of air points to the more hidden, less obviously direct powers at work in our world — the spirit of an age.

In his book *Naming the Powers,* Walter Wink provides further clarification of the nature of covert cultural forces:

> . . . the "principalities and powers" are the inner and outer aspects of any given manifestation of power. As the inner aspect they are the spirituality of institutions, the "within" of corporate structures and systems, the inner essence of outer organizations of power. . . . Every power tends to have a visible pole, an outer form — be it a church, a nation or an economy — and an invisible pole, an inner spirit or driving force that animates, legitimates, and regulates its physical manifestation in the world.[5]

He goes on to use Michael Foucault's metaphor of "epistemological space specific to a particular period," noting that "what we are dealing with here is . . . the unconscious presuppositions and world view of an entire era."[6]

Hegemony is a sphere of influence, such as has been exercised by the United States over Latin America or by the former Soviet Union over Eastern Europe. The notion of hegemony expands our awareness of the myriad factors at work in the process of control and domination: economics, politics, the military, media, education, and religion. It often involves the mechanisms of force, ideology, and culture. For example, the United States' control over Latin America

5. Walter Wink, *Naming the Powers* (Minneapolis: Augsburg/Fortress, 1982), p. 5.
6. Wink, *Naming the Powers,* p. 7.

involves the use of economic force, such as "structural adjustment": trade policies, international banking, and debt reduction programs. It has also often involved the military, as in our invasions of Guatemala, the Dominican Republic, Grenada, Mexico, Panama, and Puerto Rico, and our support of the military or paramilitary.

But to limit our understanding of the mechanisms of control to economic, political, and military force is to miss other vital elements: the ideological and broadly cultural factors. There has been a strong, overt ideology of anti-communism and pro-capitalism throughout Latin America. U.S. governmental agencies such as AID and Voice of America have conveyed this ideology through the media. Christianity has been at the forefront of that anti-communist ideological indoctrination, especially in its fundamentalist Protestant forms, though at times Roman Catholicism has not been far behind. This ideology supports U.S. influence and control throughout the region.

There have also been many covert messages that reinforce U.S. hegemony. In even the most remote villages of Latin America one finds at least one television set, often in the public plaza. People are seduced weekly by the lure of capitalism in soap operas, movies, commercials, and other showcases for the American way of life. Comic books regularly portray the superiority, desirability, and inevitable victory of the "American way of life." Billboards and magazines solicit consumption as the means to the good life. Everywhere one turns in Latin America, there are subtle messages from the United States that shape both private and public life.

The churches in Latin America have also carried out this covert influence. They have become the bearers of a certain religious way of thinking about life that allows U.S. hegemony to go unchallenged. Much of the Christianity that the West has exported to Latin America has emphasized a purely internal salvation that is a private matter between God and the individual; its primary purpose is to prepare one's soul for eternal life in another realm after death. In its most extreme forms, this theology is a significant factor in inducing docility and passivity among its adherents. If all that really matters is life after death, then it is neither important nor appropriate to engage in hopes and struggles related to current policies and events. Such passivity plays into the hands of the ruling elite, both in its internal oligarchic form and in its foreign neo-colonial form.

To speak of hegemony is to recognize the holistic nature of the mechanisms of domination, including the unintentional, the indirect, and the covert. Of these less direct mechanisms of control, religious practices and beliefs have emerged as extremely important.

Religious Beliefs and Hegemony

It was in this regard that Max Weber saw the influence of Protestantism upon the development of capitalism.[7] It is not, according to Weber, that Protestantism set out to provide an ideological justification for capitalism, but rather that in developing its notion of the "call" and in accounting for signs of election it gave rise to a "spirit" conducive to capitalism. Its influence was unintentional but significant.

For Weber, the new element that Protestantism introduced into the culture was related to the vocation of the Christian. Because Protestants understood their service to God to be through their vocation *(per vocatione)* rather than simply while carrying out their vocation *(in vocatione),* the secular arena was just as much the means to God's service as the religious arena. Accordingly, the Christian who was engaged in secular work was responsible to do the very best possible in order to glorify God through that work. This meant that one was responsible to work diligently and to earn as much as possible. This shift from the Roman Catholic notion that one served God best through the religious realm to the Lutheran understanding that one served God by living the secular life in a manner that was religious was carried one step further by Calvin. Calvin's notion that one served God best by being the best at whatever one did provided a rational obligation for the businessperson to make money. For the first

7. Max Weber, *The Protestant Ethic and the Spirit of Capitalism* (New York: Charles Scribner's Sons, 1958), esp. Chapters 3-5.

time in history, according to Weber, humans had a moral obligation to make money.

But Calvin also believed that responsibility before God involved a tempered asceticism. The godly person was not given to ostentatious display or massive accumulation for its own sake. Rather, we are granted the fruits of our labor for the purpose of glorifying God through acts of charity and kindness. This led not only to significant generosity, but also to accumulation of money that could neither be spent on oneself nor totally given away. The surplus provided a source of capital for new investments and, under normal circumstances, the cycle of moneymaking repeated itself.

Weber noted one other factor in Protestantism's contribution to the spirit of capitalism. Protestantism, in its critique and correction of Roman Catholicism, emphasized the accountability of the individual before God, unmediated by the church. The sacraments, which for Roman Catholicism were a guarantee of one's right relationship with God, were interpreted more as memorials and symbols rather than as institutionally controlled certifiers of the state of one's soul. With the removal of the sacraments as the sign of salvation, Protestants were left with the question, "How can I be sure I am saved?" At this point the notion that riches are an assurance of God's blessing offered an answer. They are a sign of God's election. This further intensified the desire of the Protestant to make as much money as possible, in order to have a sign of assurance.

Weber has been criticized for setting forth a simplistic theory that attributes too great a role to Protestant theology while failing to account for other determining factors (such as the rise of modern accounting procedures), that fails to recognize similar capitalistic developments in regions under the influence of Roman Catholicism, and that relies too heavily upon narrow understandings of Protestantism largely related to English Puritanism.[8] But despite the accu-

---

8. For an analysis and critique of Weber's thesis see Robert W. Green, ed., *Protestantism, Capitalism and Social Science: The Weber Thesis Controversy,* 2nd ed. (Lexington, MA: Heath and Co., 1973).

racy of these criticisms, his thesis that Protestantism gave rise to a spirit that supported a burgeoning capitalism has proven accurate enough to remain at the center of the debate about the relationship between religion and capitalism. And his argument has pointed to the complexity of the relationship between ideas and structures, between culture and economics.

Throughout history, similar connections between religious teachings or practices and the broader public life have become evident. One of the most glaring recent cases of the hegemonic role of Christian religion is the Holocaust. At the ideological level, Nazi propaganda utilized Christian theology as justification for anti-Judaism. But the subtler and more covert hegemonic role of Christian theology was even more influential and critical in supporting Hitler's catastrophic tragedy. The Nazis could not have made such a blatantly ideological case based on Christian theology had it not been part of the German atmosphere. There was a spirit of the times at work — a spirit of anti-Judaism — that provided a foundation for the Nazi propaganda. Without a soil ready for the seed, the seed would not have taken root. Such flagrantly racist and inhuman claims would not have been received by the German people had there not been a spirit of anti-Judaism alive in the larger culture and religious community.

As Darrell J. Fasching has documented, overt anti-Jewish claims have been present throughout the church's history, from earliest times.[9] The Jews were identified as "Christ killers" (Justin Martyr), "animals fit for slaughter" (Chrysostom), and as people who "whore after other gods" (Luther). Some of these claims, especially the allegation that it was the Jews who killed Jesus, served as grist for the ideological mill. But there was an even more subtle and pervasive root to the anti-Judaism that permeated the church and Nazi Germany. While its original intent was not to create demonic anti-Jewish sentiments, it nonetheless had that effect. Fasching sees a direct con-

9. Darrell Fasching, *Narrative Theology After Auschwitz: From Alienation to Ethics* (Minneapolis: Augsburg/Fortress, 1992).

nection between a form of anti-Judaism that never intended to support genocidal policies and a spirit that made such genocide possible:

> Based on the myth of supersession, which has its roots in the New Testament literature, the Christian claim has been that Christ has brought a "new covenant" that replaces the old (e.g., Heb. 8). Therefore the people of the Mosaic covenant have no right to exist as God's chosen people. By claiming that election was transferred from the people of Israel to the community of the new covenant, Christians have engaged in a process of spiritual genocide. . . . The step from such spiritual genocide to physical genocide — from "you have no right to exist as Jews" to "you have no right to exist" is a step prepared by Christian *religious* anti-Judaism and carried out under Nazi *secular* anti-Semitism.[10]

Both Weber and Fasching have made a strong case for the role of Christian theology in preparing and fertilizing the ground for secular, public behaviors. While there were elements of open, ideological use of theology, the more important role it played was in establishing a spirit of the times, an atmosphere in which certain attitudes and activities could flourish. Both utilized a similar method; they began by examining public, secular policies and practices and sought the possible connection between those policies and practices and the role of Christian theology. What captured Weber's attention was the qualitatively different form capitalism had taken in modern Western society — a change so enormous that it developed new "types, forms and directions."[11] In particular, what was new to modern capitalism was the "rational capitalistic organization of (formally) free labor."[12] Two things are important here. First, Weber understood the accuracy of Marx's allegation that the worker, under capitalism, was no longer

10. Fasching, *Narrative Theology After Auschwitz,* p. 21.
11. Weber, *Protestant Ethic,* p. 20.
12. Weber, *Protestant Ethic,* p. 21.

free. While he differed from Marx at many points, most especially with respect to the role of ideas in the making of history, he certainly agreed that contemporary capitalism had divided the world into owners and workers in a manner that shackled the working class. The second distinguishing characteristic of modern capitalism was that it rationalized the organization of greed and acquisitiveness. It was here that Weber made his unique contribution, asserting that this rationale was substantially rooted in an ethos or spirit created by Protestant theology.

Similarly, Fasching — following in the steps of other Christian theologians such as Rosemary Radford Ruether and Franklin Littell — began his reflection with the horror of the Holocaust. The death of millions of Jews and others at the hands of the Nazis is a fact of contemporary Western "civilization" that will not allow us to do theology as usual. With this willingness to ask new questions and accept no assumptions, Fasching began to explore the religious roots of this horror. For Fasching, the most important truth to grasp is the manner in which Christian theology, since the early church, has provided an anti-Jewish ethos that allowed and helped give rise to such horror. In these two cases, the rise of capitalism and the cataclysm of the Holocaust, we have specific instances of the way in which Christian theology not only provided ideological rationalization but also created a spirit, an ethos, an atmosphere that became part of the hegemony.

Cornel West has documented the often unconscious process of hegemonic collusion in his study of the "genealogy of modern racism." He traces the way in which the scientific stance of observation coupled with the Greek notion of beauty went hand in hand with a developing deprecation of blacks and the rise of the assumption of white supremacy. The important thing to notice about that process is that ". . . the initial structure of modern discourse in the West 'secretes' the idea of white supremacy."[13] To secrete may mean either to conceal or to release or distribute, as in a poison gas. In this case it can mean both. While ideology is usually overt and often so palpably ob-

13. West, *Prophesy Deliverance*, p. 48.

vious that it sometimes is labeled "propaganda," cultural influences are often so subtle as to go unnoticed. They are often concealed. Nonetheless, they deliver an impact — they release a spirit. When we speak of hegemony, we are dealing with a reality in which indirect and often obtuse linkages are present, not simply immediately evident correlations.

This trinity of force, ideology, and cultural secretion (what I call "inspiriting") has been at work in all of the important historic and contemporary forms of domination and control in Western society. The roles played by force and ideologies are usually fairly obvious. For example, in the case of plantation slavery, direct force was used to capture and transport Africans for slavery and, once here, to keep them on the plantations; physical violence, laws, and economic controls were used to enforce their slave status. At the same time, there was also a clear ideological justification offered for the role of Africans as slaves. The science of phrenology depicted Africans as inferior due to the size and slope of their foreheads. Sociologically, certain human attributes were ascribed as essential to specific races. The Bible was also used to reinforce the inferiority of the black race. Many taught that the curse of the black race was directly related to the sin of Ham. Ham, the youngest son of Noah, witnessed the nakedness of his father who had fallen asleep drunk. Rather than covering him, Ham went out and brought his two older brothers to see him. They refused to look at their father, walking in backward and covering him. When Noah heard what Ham had done, he cursed him and his descendants, the tribe of Canaan, with these words: "Cursed be Canaan; a slave of slaves shall he be to his brothers" (Gen. 9:25). This curse was assumed to be upon all black people from that time forward. The Apostle Paul's mandate that slaves be obedient to their masters (Col. 3:22) was another biblical text that served the ideological cause well. Force and ideology combined to suppress blacks in the condition of slavery.

It was the same for women. Force was often used to keep women "in their place": the Salem witch trials and burnings, the withholding of the vote, the economic law that gave control of all assets to the husband in the case of divorce, and in many other instances as well. Women also faced the overt ideological use of science and Scripture. Evolutionary terms were used to describe women as the weaker sex. Biblically, the account of the temptation and fall of Adam and Eve was assumed to mean that Eve's punishment for her central role was to be made subservient to Adam, and hence all women to men. From the New Testament, Paul's injunction that women should be silent in the church was used as a rationale to keep women out of leadership roles. Sexism has been maintained by both force and ideology.

In the oppression of homosexuals force has been a constant reality: muggings and burning at the stake, legal prohibitions, imprisonment, and ostracisms. And there has been direct ideological use of Scripture, such as the Hebrew Scripture's prohibition in the Holiness Codes, which refers to male homosexual acts as an abomination, or Paul's castigation of "unnatural acts" in Romans 1. Heterosexism too has been maintained by both force and ideology.

Inspiriting and Oppressions

As I have visited and participated in churches of all kinds, I have noticed that even those that don't have a grasp on the ideology of Scripture and have not directly participated in enforcing racism, sexism, or heterosexism nonetheless have a "biblical" theology that grounds their responses. It is not a well-articulated theology, nor is it necessarily consistent in terms of Scripture or coherent within its own development. It is more like a biblical "sense." It is part of the culture and it is powerful because it secretes a spirit that shapes our responses.

It goes something like this: God made everything for a purpose, everything in its proper place. There is an order to creation and, in fact, there are orders of creation. This ordering is common sense, what some have called "natural": we have humans, then animals, then plants, then inanimate objects. For some, humans are preceded by angels. When we move into the realm of institutionalized religion, here too there are orders. At the top are the clergy, followed by the devoted women religious (in some traditions), followed by the laity. Anyone who doubts this should simply follow a member of the clergy around for a while. There is a common expectation that the clergy have a more direct pipeline to God, that their prayers count more than those of ordinary people, that they are more godly.

This sense or spirit of hierarchy carries over into other realms of life. While not necessarily designed to relegate people of color or women or gays to second-class status, this notion of orders of creation and vocation has created a spirit or ethos that makes such discrimination possible. In the orders of creation, everything has its place. And if something has its place, it is possible to be out of place. Everything is "naturally" something or somewhere, and therefore it is possible to be "unnaturally" something or somewhere. To be out of place is to be uppity, pushy, weird, deviant, or perverted — all words we have heard frequently about people of color, women, and gays and lesbians.

Hand in hand with the sense of "place" and "out of place" is the sense of ontological superiority. Certain places are preferable or superior to others. Angels are superior to people, people to animals, and so forth. This easily gets broken down even further, with many believing that men are superior to women, whites to blacks, those who are "straight" to those who are gay, clergy to laity, and on and on. I suspect that it is this general sense about the ordering or hierarchy of creation, more than any one argument from Scripture or any single theological doctrine, that supports contemporary racism, sexism, and heterosexism. Because this general sense is a spirit in the air we breathe, even when unarticulated it has power to shape our responses. This is what I call the inspiriting power of religion. You don't have to be Jewish to love Levy's bread, you don't have to be Christian to sing "Amazing Grace," and you don't have to be theologically aware or intentional to be influenced by the spirit of a theology that has become part of the secular air we breathe.

When we turn to our penal system and its punitive nature, we have the same three factors at work: force, ideology, and cultural inspiriting. It is obvious that the punishment that characterizes our penal system is carried out and maintained by force. Most visible in the enforcement role are the police, with their nightsticks, handcuffs, and guns. At times, the use of force by the police becomes inordinate even by the standards of a punitive society. When Amadou Diallo was shot at forty-three times and hit by twenty-seven of the bullets fired or Abner Louima was anally assaulted with a broom handle in the police station, many people rose to protest. Even normally unconcerned citizens voiced their anger as Mayor Rudolph Giuliani and the police officials tried to stonewall the tragedy. Many carried out acts of civil disobedience in an effort to force a serious response from the government to the police brutality.

The enforcement of our penal system goes beyond the police: laws, courts, jails, and prisons all play their role. Certain laws are guaranteed to target people of color and the poor. Targeting crack, a cheap street drug, rather than cocaine, a luxury drug used primarily by whites in middle- and upper-class settings, has resulted in a disproportionate number of arrests of the poor and people of color.

Ideology also undergirds our punitive response to crime. Certain crimes are considered "dirtier" than others. Breaking and entering often receives harsher sentences than embezzlement, though the amount of money involved might be astronomically greater in the case of embezzlement. Some attribute criminal behavior to genetic traits possessed by certain races more than others. Some lives are considered more valuable than others. According to the Death Penalty Information Center, "almost all capital cases (84%) involve white victims, even though 50% of murder victims are black."[14] The center's study goes on to quote the U.S. General Accounting Office as saying, "In 82% of the cases reviewed, race of the victim was found to influence the likelihood of being charged with capital murder or receiving the death penalty, i.e., those who murder whites were found more likely to be sentenced to death than those who murder blacks." There is an ideology that supports our current punitive response to crime, and it is largely related to the ideology of racism.

14. "Facts About the Death Penalty," Death Penalty Information Center newsletter, March 27, 1995, p. 2.

In addition to the use of force and ideology, our punitive response to crime is reinforced by a spirit of punishment. It is a subtle spirit, many-layered and often hard to grasp. One of the foundations of this spirit, I have come to believe, is a distortion of the Christian notion of grace, a distortion that is largely Protestant in its origins. This distortion is not *the* foundation of that spirit, but it is part of the foundation. It is not more important than the factors of force and ideology, nor more important than other, nonreligious culturally inspiriting factors, but it is as important.

The church is responsible in every age to examine its teachings and its practices to determine their impact upon the marginal, the weak, and the oppressed. Often doctrines or practices that are life giving in one situation are destructive in another. The necessary self-protection that occupied the early church in the days of persecution is not an appropriate response for a church that lives comfortably with the powers that be. The emphasis upon the individual that challenged a monopoly power of the Roman Catholic Church in the sixteenth century must not be the emphasis at a time when rampant individualism threatens to destroy all concern for community and the commonweal. It is incumbent upon the church to continually be alert to the positive and negative power of its life. That is why Calvin and other Reformers insisted upon a church that was "Reformed, but always reforming." I therefore invite those who care about the church's role in contemporary life to look at the ways in which the popular understanding of grace may unwittingly reinforce the spirit of punishment that characterizes our society.

| | |

CHAPTER TWO

Grace Isn't Only for Wretches

"Amazing Grace, how sweet the sound
that saved a wretch like me."

Grace and Wretchedness

The experience that led John Newton to pen these words is one of the more dramatic conversion stories in Christian history, comparable to Paul's encounter with Jesus on the road to Damascus. Newton had lived a profligate youth, a true prodigal son. He left home, was in trouble with the law, and for a while was forced to live with a slave dealer in Africa, suffering brutality and starvation. Later, he himself became a captain of a slave trading ship, carrying Africans to bondage or death. His was a life of wretchedness and his conversion an amazing act of grace.

The epitaph he wrote for his own funeral captures the drama of the transformation in his life.

John Newton clerk
Once an Infidel and Libertine
A Servant of slaves in Africa
Was by the rich mercy of our Lord and Saviour

Jesus Christ
Preserved, restored, pardoned
And appointed to preach the Faith
He had long laboured to destroy.[1]

Written in the late 1700's, "Amazing Grace" was perhaps his most moving testimony to the transformation of his life. It was not, however, an instant success. It did not become widely popular in either England or the United States until the 1960's, when Judy Collins's version hit the secular charts. Since then, it has become as much a part of the culture as hot dogs and soda, even making its way over the loudspeaker at Veterans Stadium in Philadelphia in a 1993 National League Championship baseball game. For many, the hymn is a powerful testimony to their own experience of God's grace. It was the concluding moment of our wedding service, in gratitude and witness to the power of God's grace in our lives.

But despite its overwhelming popularity and power, there is an anomaly for most people in singing it. Most of us aren't skippers of slave ships. While only too aware of our limitations, our occasional nastiness, pettiness, or prejudice, most of us would consider ourselves to be decent folks, trying our best to be loving partners or parents, responsible members of our community, caring about those who are sick or impoverished, diligent in our work. The sense of wretchedness is not one we carry with us. The words of the confession that "there is no goodness within us" may be repeated by rote, but I doubt that they are owned by the majority who say them. What, then, is implied by singing "a wretch like me"?

As I have worked with congregations and pastors over the years, I have been struck by how widespread the perception is that God's grace is not only linked to our wretchedness but somehow dependent upon it. A young woman not noted for her church attendance was trying to honor her in-laws by going with them to their Lutheran

1. *The Hymnal 1940 Companion,* 3rd rev. ed. (New York: The Church Pension Fund, 1951), p. 515.

church. She confided to me one day that she simply had to figure out a gracious way to extricate herself from that congregation without hurting her in-laws, whom she loves. "The problem," she explained, "is that the pastor feels he has to tell us every week what terrible sinners we are in order to make God look good."

Grace and Original Sin

Protestantism tends to emphasize that grace can be understood only in relation to our understanding of sin. As Reinhold Niebuhr points out, "the Christian doctrine of grace stands in juxtaposition to the Christian doctrine of original sin and has meaning only if the latter is an accurate description of the actual facts of human experience."[2] The Protestant notion of original sin generally precludes the possibility of grace in the common actions of ordinary people. The foremost proponent of the doctrine was St. Augustine, whose struggles as a young man to overcome the temptations of the flesh fit this interpretation of Scripture. His failures led him to conclude that "I was so fallen and blinded that I could not discern the light of virtue and of beauty."[3] In a leap from the particular to the universal, he concluded that this is the plight of every human.[4] In varying ways, this emphasis was picked up by Calvin, Luther, Wesley, and other Reformers, and it

2. Reinhold Niebuhr, *The Nature and Destiny of Man*, vol. 2 (New York: Charles Scribner's Sons, 1949), p. 108.

3. *Confessions*, Book 6, Chap. XVI, p. 133, Albert C. Outler, translator and editor, from *The Library of Christian Classics*, Vol. VII, John Baillie, John T. McNeill, and Henry P. VanDusen, general editors (Philadelphia: Westminster Press, 1955), p. 133.

4. A destructive corollary of Augustine's assumption of original sin was his speculation as to the mode by which sin is transmitted from one generation to the next. Having experienced sexuality fundamentally as lust, as opposed to celebration, reciprocity, and intimacy, he asserted that the very act of intercourse itself constituted the mechanism for the transmission of original sin. His interpretation has contributed significantly to the distortion of sexuality in Western culture. For a full treatment of this see Elaine Pagels, *Adam, Eve and the Serpent* (New York: Random House, 1988).

continues to dominate much of contemporary Protestant thought through the influence of Karl Barth and neo-orthodox theology. According to this basic strain of Christianity, the unredeemed person lacks not only knowledge of God but also the capacity for such knowledge because of the fall.

Calvin understood all humanity to be tainted with sin through being born of an "impure seed" causing us to be originally depraved, and he goes on to interpret the consequence of that depravity to preclude any fundamental or salvific capacity for knowing God: "What God is in himself, and what he is in relation to us, human reason makes not the least approach."[5] Whatever residual knowledge of God, or beauty, or truth that humans possess is because of God's grace, but it is so incomplete as to result only in our condemnation. Luther indicated that Adam was the only human free to choose and that the rest of us are pawns in the hands of God and Satan.[6] John Wesley, who acknowledged that there is a prevenient grace that enables us to understand, nonetheless considered our nature utterly fallen. "Thou art corrupted in every power," he writes, "in every faculty of thy soul: thou art totally corrupted in every one of these. . . . There is no soundness in thy soul."[7] Karl Barth rejected all claims of natural theology, positing a God who is totally other, a God whom we are incapable of knowing except through the special revelation of the Holy Spirit. For each of these theologians, original sin has reduced us to utter dependence upon God's redeeming grace, without fundamental recourse to any goodness, knowledge, or capacity we possess as God's created beings.

There is an undeniable connection between sin and grace within the Christian faith, of course. It is the central claim of the Gospel that God reaches out to us in our needy condition to redeem us.

5. *The Institutes of the Christian Religion,* Book II, Vol. I, trans. Henry Beveridge (Grand Rapids: Eerdmans, 1957), p. 238.

6. Martin Luther, *Bondage of the Will,* XXV, trans. J. L. Parker and O. R. Johnston (London: J. Clark, 1957), p. 90.

7. John Wesley, *A Compend of Wesley's Theology,* ed. Robert W. Burtner and Robert E. Chiles (Nashville: Abingdon, 1954), p. 121.

Dorothee Sölle underscores the inextricable linkage between sin and grace with her claim that grace responds to the question, "How do men and women emerge from the despair and the emptiness of sin to another life?"[8]

But that is not the only function of grace. Grace not only addresses our sinful condition, it also provides the foundation for human discourse, achievement, and love. The problem arises not from acknowledging the connection between sin and redemption but from understanding sin as destroying all capacity for good, beauty, and truth. In so doing we lose sight of the grace that is present in all creation. Grace is not only about redemption, as the above quotation from Niebuhr implies and as the Reformers have stated; it is also about creation. It not only comes to us in our wretchedness — to the extent that is our condition — it also comes to us in our beauty and goodness.

Forgotten Grace: And God Said, "That's Good"

Many people fail to see grace in the ordinariness of creation. In informal interviews and questionnaires conducted with about 100 church members, non–church members, and members of other faiths, some students and I discovered that people tend to think of grace as something out of the ordinary, either an undeserved moment of redemption or an unexpected turn of events, such as a miraculous healing, a windfall, or some other one-time blessing. Grace was seen by most of those we interviewed as not only special but unusual. The idea that life itself is a result of grace was not a dominant motif. The majority spoke of grace in terms of undeserved favor, undeserved because of their sinful condition.

While all of this is true, it is not the entire truth. Grace is also ex-

---

8. Dorothee Sölle, *Thinking About God: An Introduction to Theology* (Philadelphia: Trinity Press International, 1990), p. 85.

perienced at the heart of creation, at the foundation of our everyday existence. It has to do not only with sin, but also with our life and worth. Because of the gracious gift of the creator God, we are beautiful and good. Losing sight of this has severe consequences.

This is one of the implications of Dietrich Bonhoeffer's rejection of the "God of the Gaps," the God who is met only in the foxholes, at the extremities of life's circumstances. For Bonhoeffer, God is at the center of life, in the everyday common stuff, in the creation. That is what is so unhelpful about holding up St. Paul, St. Augustine, and John Newton as *the* models of the experience of the grace of God. It can easily lead us into a competition for status as the "greatest of sinners," to make more of our wretchedness, our limitations, our needs, and our failures than perhaps is appropriate. These giants claim to have experienced God's grace at the extremity of their wretchedness. If we cannot claim to be "the greatest of sinners," where does that leave us?

Interestingly, although Paul often points to his pre-conversion state to show how dreadful his condition was and how abundant God's grace is, Paul himself warns the Christians in Rome against thinking that sin and grace are in some simple equation that might lead them to keep sinning so that they would continue to experience grace. "What then are we to say? Should we continue in sin in order that grace may abound? By no means! How can we who died to sin go on living in it?" (Rom. 6:1-2)

The connection between grace and creation, while not prominent in Protestantism, is nonetheless there. Most of us recognize the connection between grace and creation at some level. Certainly the creeds, confessions, and hymns contain references to the goodness of creation. Cecil Alexander's "All Things Bright and Beautiful," whose phrases affirming the beauty and goodness of creation have served as the titles for the James Herriot veterinary stories, has become a standard of hymnody in many churches. However, for the most part, creation seems to have been forgotten or at least to have taken a back seat. It was not always so.

James Carpenter's study of the relation of nature and grace uncovers the forgotten emphasis within the Christian tradition of the permeating presence of grace in creation. As far back as Irenaeus, Carpenter sees the affirmation of grace in each person and in all of creation:

> What Adam lost in the fall was not the *imago Dei*. By creation he was the image of God and nothing could alter this most fundamental fact of his being. But through disobedience he lost something that belonged to him by nature, and in his sin he became unnatural. He lost the *similtudo Dei,* lost the freedom to be like God, and with this lost incorruptibility and immortality, that which essentially denoted likeness to God.[9]

Carpenter captures Irenaeus' and other Eastern theologians' sense that "the fall into sin did not result in gracelessness; it resulted in the diminution of the effect of grace."[10] He contrasts this with what he characterizes as Augustine's and Western theology's sense of the separation between nature and grace: "Nature . . . is without grace until graced by redemption. Behind it lay Augustine's insistence that grace deserted the first parents upon their disobedience."[11]

James Muilenburg discovered the same truth within the Scriptures themselves more than fifty years ago. In his study of the *imago Dei,* he asks,

> Just how corrupt is he (man)? . . . What is important . . . is the actual biblical portrait of a man in relation to the fall. First, it should be observed that man continues to be described as the image of God after the fall. . . . What is significant to the historian of religion is that the Priestly writer responsible for the Pentateuch in its final form ignores the fall completely and is totally unaware of any hereditary implications. . . . What is re-

9. James Carpenter, *Nature and Grace: Toward an Integral Perspective* (New York: Crossroad, 1988), p. 23.

10. Carpenter, *Nature and Grace,* p. 30.

11. Carpenter, *Nature and Grace,* p. 8.

markable about the story of the fall is that nowhere in the Old Testament is it used as the basis for man's corruption. Indeed, nowhere in the Old Testament (nor in the New!) do we have so dark a picture of man's corruption as is painted by Martin Luther and Karl Barth.[12]

The anthropology of the black churches, for the most part, has followed this same pattern — it has not succumbed to a thoroughly dualistic conception. While slavery and racism have forced black preachers and theologians to acknowledge the radical nature of sin, they somehow have been able to keep sight of the fundamental presence of the *imago Dei*. This recognition has enabled them to affirm the kinship and equality of all people.[13] This almost unfathomable ability to affirm the humanity of one's oppressors is one of the most significant challenges to the contemporary spirit of punishment.

Contemporary liberation theology has also affirmed the capacity for goodness, beauty, and truth within all people. Again, while holding to a radical understanding of sin and the need for redemption, Leonardo Boff sets forth an understanding of grace as dialogical, as involving reciprocity between God and humans. For Boff, there is an assumed capacity within humans for correct desire and correct choice:

> Described in terms of nature, these two images of God and the human being (grace and nature) do not succeed in communicating the dialogical reality of God and humans, which is characterized by freedom, gratuitousness, and an openness to the other. Grace is not just God, not just the human being. It is the encounter of the two, each giving of self and opening up to the other.[14]

12. James Muilenburg, "Imago Dei," *Review of Religion* 7 (May 1942): 397-98.
13. Peter Paris, *The Social Teachings of the Black Churches* (Philadelphia: Fortress, 1985), p. 11.
14. Leonardo Boff, *Liberating Grace* (Maryknoll, NY: Orbis, 1988), p. 17.

If grace is not so inextricably linked with our falseness (that is, not seen only in terms of redemption), we are opened up to the possibility present within the broader Catholic, Orthodox, black church, and liberation traditions insisting on the goodness, beauty, worth and moral capacity in everyone God has created. That is, grace is present and at work within all of human experience. Life is graceful. We need not focus on the fall to recognize the presence of grace.

The Ecological Consequences of the Loss of Creation Grace

The importance of the recovery of grace in creation cannot be overstated, for the absence of a sense of the graciousness of creation has had severe consequences not only for humans but for the environment as well. Contemporary technological and industrial society has been shaped largely without reference to or an understanding of God's grace being present within nature. Having lost sight of the graciousness of nature, it has been an easy step for many to view nature as purely functional, existing for the sake of human purposes alone. Nature is there to be used, dominated, and controlled.

James Nash has provided a realistic picture of the ecological crisis we face. Without falling into sloganeering and apocalyptic despair, he offers a balanced presentation, affirming the basic direction of the Club of Rome's warnings offered in the early 1970's *(The Limits to Growth)* but allowing for the possibility of corrections available through technological progress. Most striking, for our purposes, is his documentation of the complicity of Christian theology to treat nature merely as a subsidiary to or function of human history. Summing up, he says,

> For most theologians — Augustine to Luther, Aquinas to Barth, and the bulk of the others in between and before and after — the theological focus has been on sin and salvation, the fall and redemption, the divine-human relationship over against the

biophysical world as a whole. The focus has been overwhelmingly on human history to the neglect of natural history . . . thereby [giving] tacit (rarely explicit) permission for environmental destruction to proceed as an ultimately and morally immaterial matter.[15]

Echoing a similar concern, Sallie McFague critiques what she describes as the monarchical model of God, which is both hierarchical and dualistic. That model, she says, "is dangerous in our time: it encourages a sense of distance from the world; it attends only to the human dimension of the world; and it supports attitudes of either domination of the world or passivity toward it."[16] In contrast, she seeks models that offer us a more connected understanding of God and the creation, suggesting that the world is "God's body." The implications of this are striking, both for the way we regard nature in general and the way we regard human beings in particular.

No one can deny that treating nature functionally as a resource for human life has born valuable fruits. Medicines have been discovered or created that have provided cures or even eliminated certain diseases; waterways have been turned into energy and irrigation sources; the airwaves have been used for communication; space exploration has conquered limits long thought fixed. That is the good news.

This functional approach to nature has brought tragedy as well. It has led to the rape of the environment, the destruction of the atmosphere, the elimination or endangerment of entire species, and the creation of nuclear and chemical weapons of mass destruction. The human species is now threatened with the potential of being overtaken by global warming, being poisoned by polluted air and water, or blowing itself to smithereens.

The failure to recognize the intrinsic — as opposed to the purely

15. James Nash, *Loving Nature: Ecological Integrity and Christian Responsibility* (Nashville: Abingdon, 1991), p. 72.

16. Sallie McFague, *Models of God: Theology for an Ecological Nuclear Age* (Philadelphia: Fortress Press, 1987), p. 69.

functional — value of nature has become one of the most important subjects in the field of ethics. There has been a marked increase of interest in environmental ethics and environmental theology during the last twenty-five years. The *Religion Index for Periodical Literature* indicates that while between 1967 and 1972 there were approximately 50 articles written concerning ethical or theological reflections on the environment, nature, or ecology, between 1987 and 1992 there were more than 350 — a sevenfold increase. Significantly, a number of the current articles point out that one of the fundamental roots of our contemporary environmental threat is precisely the failure to treat nature as an integral part of the whole life process, as "God's body." We are a part of it and it a part of us. The objectification of nature as "other" has blinded us to the truth of our mutual reciprocity with it. The reductionistic focus on redemption to which Nash refers is one of the most fundamental reasons why the Christian churches have served as the largely uncritical handmaidens and butlers of the scientific method — an essentially utilitarian approach. And the results of that utilitarianism have been devastating.

If It Has Devastated Nature, What Has It Done to People?

When we divorce grace from creation, it is possible not only to treat the environment as a thing to be used, but also to treat persons as things with only functional value. If not all of creation is the bearer of God's grace, then it follows that some of creation stands outside the purview of grace, fallen from the image of God and therefore inferior in the order of things. It then becomes possible to treat persons as "other" and to objectify them into non-personhood. Nowhere can this be seen more clearly than within our penal system and the general public's response to criminals.

The chilling introduction to *Life Sentences: Race and Survival Behind Bars* provides us with a sobering account of our potential inhumanity as it describes the Louisiana State Executioner. "Sam" (an alias) has killed 19 people in the electric chair, receiving $400 for each execution. Noting the impersonality and efficiency of the killings, the authors quote Sam as saying, "There's nothin' to it. It's no different to me executing somebody and goin' to the refrigerator and getting a beer out of it."[17]

Sam's matter-of-factness is only different in degree, not in kind, from many people with whom I have come in contact, and resonates with my own feelings at times. In 1987 a woman who rented an apartment in our home was raped at knifepoint. The assailant, a slight man, bent the bars on the windows and crawled through an eight-inch opening. We were home at the time but unaware of the tragedy going on in our own house. When the rapist had left, the tenant called us on the phone and we rushed to see her. My first reaction was to try to find the man and kill him.

Pure instinct? Perhaps, but I doubt it. My reaction was conditioned by years of television, hosts of friends who spoke similarly of what should be done to criminals, and the police, who routinely spoke of such persons as the scum of the earth, garbage, or worse. I have heard similar responses from people across the political spectrum, both within the church and without. There is a spirit of punishment alive in the land, a spirit that makes us quick to judge, quick to imagine the worst, quick to desire retribution and vengeance.

However, there is a difference between an immediate, personal, visceral response and a studied, structured, institutionalized process, which is what our penal system is intended to be. Even at the personal level, time and distance may alter the initial visceral response. Questions may begin to emerge about the assailant's own life and circumstances. While there can be no excuse for brutality, we may come to an understanding that there are more appropriate ways to deal with the assailant than killing or maiming — ways that might lead to healing and change. Such time, distance, and reflection are ostensibly the hallmarks of the criminal justice system in this country. Lawyers, investigations, and trials are all intended to provide for a deliberative

17. Wilbert Rideau and Ron Wikberg, eds., *Life Sentences: Race and Survival Behind Bars* (New York: Times Books, 1992), p. 5.

process, so that emotions and crowd behavior do not dictate the response, so that justice can prevail. Yet that is seldom the result. The penal system and our personal responses are often the same — vindictive and clamoring for punishment. My response to the rapist was understandable, if not laudatory. The response of the penal system is indefensible.

One of the most egregious aspects of our criminal justice system is its lack of evenhandedness. Often, white-collar crimes that deprive tens of thousands of people of millions of dollars often do not result in a jail sentence, while street crimes entailing far smaller amounts — often involving breaking and entering — elicit stern sentences. In October 1993 a *New York Times* article posited three possible reasons. At the top of the list was "the assumption that such violators are basically good people who stepped over a line but are not really criminals. Prosecutors have limited resources, and criminal fraud cases are hard to prove. The public demand is to do something about crime in the streets, not crime in the suites."[18]

This uneven response to crime is cause enough for consternation. But an even greater tragedy is that the fundamental response to street crime is to view the criminal, in most cases, as something less than human, as a "thing." The attitude of "Sam" mentioned above is a cruder but accurate example of the broader society's response.

This objectification of marginal persons has many precedents. Some of the harshest criticisms of industrial capitalism were directed at the production line, where the worker was viewed as little more than an extension of the machinery. It was this objectification that enabled people to accept the practice of child labor that was so prevalent in early industrial capitalism and is still widespread in the global economy.

Women too have been objectified and exploited systematically. The prostitution industry is largely a reduction of sexual relations to a monetary transaction between two objects. Advertising has been notorious for its use of women's bodies to sell products. Ironically, in

18. *New York Times,* Oct. 3, 1993, section 3, p. 1.

a move toward gender equality, the advertising industry has given us mostly naked men in provocative poses as well, selling everything from underwear to fragrances.

The old-fashioned assembly lines have been reinvented in the current era of downsizing and factory relocation. Workers have become interchangeable. Many businesses simply seek the cheapest labor anywhere in the world, with no sense of obligation to people who have worked for them for years and who helped to create their wealth. As a result, the historic loyalty that many workers felt toward their employers has been shattered. When workers' lives are so traumatically affected by decisions about the bottom line, they often bitterly come to realize that they are merely pawns in an economic game.

Whether treated as criminal trash, extensions of machines, sex objects, or economic pawns, increasing numbers of persons within our society are experiencing the tragedy of objectification and utilitarian treatment. They know what it is like to be considered devoid of worth, dignity, and beauty.

Grace, the Objectification of Persons, and Racism

In the same way that failure to recognize the grace inherent within creation has contributed to an objectified or functionalist attitude toward nature, it has done so to persons as well. The particular Augustinian/Protestant notion of sin as a fall into perdition and of grace understood only or primarily in terms of redemption contributes to treating persons as objects in the same manner that it does with respect to nature — not as the only factor, of course, but as part of the reinforcement of a spirit.

Once we have a category into which to fit people, they can be objectified. We are familiar with the classifications of slave and free, black and white, cowboys and "Indians," men and women, etc. These classifications, based upon empirical observation, are often turned into ontological categories that divide people not just in terms of functions but also in terms of their essential being. The assumption of essential difference is what enables persons to be thought of and treated as inferior, as objects, as purely functional, leading to or reinforcing larger structures of alienation and disease.

The classifications of "fallen" and "redeemed" — understood in reference to essential being and not simply in reference to behavior — serve as a way to divide the human race into persons and "nonpersons." This high doctrine of sin, articulated above in relation to the consequences of the fall, results in what Tom Driver has called "the latent Christian doctrine of the nonperson."[19] Some are unworthy, and evil, and others are graced. Some are alive; others are dead. Some are of God and some are of Satan. When we use these classifications within a society already divided by the classifications and structures of racism, there is an easy if not necessarily intentional fit.

The classifications of redeemed and unredeemed predate Western racism, of course, and it is not only Protestants with a high doctrine of sin who have participated in that racism. It is not that the Protestant notion of sin and grace has single-handedly or intentionally created Western racism, but it has played into its hands easily and indirectly. Just as the Protestant notion of calling did not serve as the single and all-sufficient cause of the rise of modern capitalism, so too the Protestant understanding of grace is not solely responsible for the objectification of human beings and the racism that it reinforces. The roots of that mentality run far deeper than simply a particular Christian attitude.

But the Protestant notion of sin as a fall from grace has fed into and contributed to racism, one of the most fundamental and insidious aspects of Western modernity. We can see this in the founding and development of our nation, which had many blatantly racist overtones. In the context of that racism, distinctions between sinner and saved easily became part of its undergirding right from the beginning of the European conquest of the continent. When one be-

19. Tom F. Driver, *Christ in a Changing World: Toward an Ethical Christology* (New York: Crossroads, 1981), p. 58.

lieves that all people — except for those who have been redeemed — are heathen, living in darkness, and lost in perdition, it is easy to justify treating them as objects rather than as persons.

The literature of our early settlement period is filled with allusions to Native Americans as less than human. In one of the most complete and definitive studies of Native Americans, Robert F. Berkhofer Jr. documents the common conception of whites that Native Americans were "alien and other."[20] This sense of otherness was reinforced by the understanding that they were "deficient in the virtues, values and habits" of the European settlers. This sense of deficiency was coupled with a notion of the Indian as a savage, devoid of human sensitivities. Even as many Europeans recognized that Native Americans had souls, they considered them degenerate, lower on the hierarchy of human development. This cultural foundation, which incorporated a religious judgment that Native Americans were heathens, was combined with the sciences of anthropology and biology to produce a full-blown scientific racism that resulted in Native Americans being adopted as wards of the state and prohibited from citizenship until 1924. The economic, political and military roots and structures of our genocidal relationship with Native Americans were accompanied and reinforced by an attitude that considered Native Americans to be less than fully human, to be treated as such until and unless they converted to Christianity.

Brutality and genocidal policies toward blacks throughout our history have been of similar magnitude. Treated as chattel, constitutionally described as only partially human (three fifths), auctioned like cattle, and exploited as machines for fieldwork and procreation, black slaves were systematically denied their humanity. The same denigration, but in different form, continued apace under the Jim Crow laws of Reconstruction, urban ghettoization, unemployment and welfare, police brutality, and the penal system. Through many

20. Robert F. Berkhofer Jr., "White Conceptions of Indians," in *Handbook of North American Indians,* vol. 4: *History of Indian-White Relations,* ed. Wilcomb E. Washburn (Washington: Smithsonian Institution, 1988), p. 522.

manifestations of racism, blacks have been systematically treated as inhuman or less than human. Ralph Ellison captured the essence of that objectification and denigration in his novel *The Invisible Man*. Echoing the theme of the title, Ellison writes of the dynamics between Mr. Norton, a wealthy white member of the board of trustees of a black college, and the hero of the novel, who is at that point a student: "Poor stumblers, neither of you can see the other. To you [Mr. Norton] he is a mark on the scorecard of your achievement, a thing and not a man; a child, or even less — a black amorphous thing."[21]

It may seem like a long stretch from a doctrine of grace exclusively or principally understood in terms of redemption and the kind of overt, brutal racism described above, but the linkage is fairly clear. When we consider all persons as innately sinful (by virtue of their birth into a fallen condition), then we have a category in which to fit them: lost sinners, reprobates, ungodly. If we then add the possibility that God has reached out and lifted some out of that condition, we then add a second category: the redeemed. Make no mistake; in basic Protestant theology these two categories are *essentially* different. Those in the first are doomed to eternal death or punishment; those in the second are participants in glorious eternal life. While it is God's grace that makes the difference, not any merit on the part of the redeemed, there is nonetheless a fundamental or essential difference between the two classifications — a difference as distinctive as day and night, as life and death. White Christians viewed black slaves as the unredeemed and lost, who could therefore be treated differently than the redeemed. This treatment fit very neatly with the general secular understanding of blacks as animal-like, as less than human, as ugly, as inferior in every respect.

White Christians taught a theology to blacks that continually reinforced their subordinate and qualitatively different status in the hierarchy of God's world. One of the ways in which this reinforcement was carried out was through the catechetical process. There were

21. Ralph Ellison, *The Invisible Man* (New York: Signet Books, 1952), p. 87.

separate catechisms for slaves. One of the more popular ones, "A Catechism for Negroes," whose authorship was attributed to "A Lady," was circulated in the *Southern Episcopalian*. Alongside the traditional elements in the catechisms for white people are several phrases that clearly sought to instill a sense of worthlessness in slaves:

> *What makes you lazy?*
> My own wicked heart . . .

> *What makes you curse and fight?*
> My own wicked heart . . .

> *How do you know your heart is wicked?*
> I feel it every day . . .

> *Who teaches you so many wicked things?*
> The Devil.[22]

References to laziness, cursing, and fighting are largely relegated to the slaves and not the slaveholders. In the same issue of the journal, a missionary at Calvary Church in Charleston, South Carolina states that, in addition to the normal obstacles posed by evil hearts in all people, the slaves possessed "strong sensual propensities and the fearful corresponding temptations, which seem to be inherent in the natures, and certainly beset the steps of the young of both sexes, and especially of the females, in this class of people."[23]

That white racism is rooted in a fabric woven of far more threads than simply the division of redeemed and unredeemed is evidenced by the fact that so many white Christians continued to treat as slaves any blacks who converted. The spirit of racism ran too deep to be erased simply by religious conversion. Perhaps none of us is so pure that we would not fall into the trap of objectification and denigration

---

22. "A Catechism for Negroes," *The Southern Episcopalian,* April 1, 1854, p. 7.
23. *The Southern Episcopalian,* April 1, 1854, p. 9.

even if a grace-filled creation were part of our doctrinal underpinning. But the absence of a doctrine of creation grace simply provides more foundation for the idea that some people do not possess the requisites to consider them intrinsically worthy, beautiful, and good.

Creation Grace as Relationship

When we view persons as intrinsically worthy, beautiful, and good, it becomes easier for us to avoid objectification and denigration. Confucius, for example, had a different way of treating those whom he considered to be straying from the path. Despite their deviation from what he considered right or normal or appropriate, he saw in them an innate goodness to which he constantly responded. Baron Chi K'ang Tsu once asked Confucius,

> "Ought not I to cut off the lawless in order to establish law and order? What do you think?" . . . Confucius [replied], "Sir, what need is there of the death penalty in your system of government? If you showed a sincere desire to be good, your people would likewise be good. The virtue of the prince is like unto wind; that of the people like unto the grass. For it is the nature of grass to bend when the wind blows upon it."[24]

Jesus, like Confucius, understood that the pervasive and subtle cultural impact of living by example would be even greater than any overt mandates of law and punishment. Perhaps that is why Jesus was not fixated upon the law, as many in his day were, but rather modeled deeds of loving-kindness, a spirit of forgiveness, and a willingness to put people before the law. He understood that by eating with publicans and sinners, by touching the untouchables, by talking with those who were outcasts, he was undermining the very

24. As quoted by John B. Noss and David S. Noss, *Man's Religions,* 7th ed. (New York: Macmillan, 1984), p. 275.

foundation of the dominant society with its hierarchical privileges and injustices. In Jesus' day there was an entire category of people who were considered objects of revulsion and rejection. These were the sick and the poor, thought to be justly suffering God's punishment for their sinfulness. The story of the man Jesus healed who was blind from birth reveals a common attitude toward such persons. "Rabbi," the disciples asked Jesus, "who sinned, this man or his parents, that he was born blind?" (John 9:2). If he is poor and sick, it must be because of someone's sin. Jesus' followers asked such a question, not unbelievers, cynics, or enemies. They shared the pervasive attitude of the time.

Jesus' response rejected the classification of the man as simply an object — a sinner, or blind man, or outcast. The father of a child who has Down's syndrome taught me a lesson I am still learning. Each time I referred to someone as "a Down's syndrome baby" or a "blind man" he would correct me and say, "Put the baby or the man first, not the illness or difficulty. Do not define people by their condition but by their humanity." Jesus saw the man born blind as a child of God, possessing worth. It was not so much what Jesus said as what he did that shows the fundamentally different attitude he had toward the man who was blind. He made mud, placed it on his eyes, and addressed him directly. The disciples could only talk *about* the man. Jesus talked *to* him. The disciples kept their distance. Jesus touched him. Jesus refused to classify people on the basis of some notion of sin: the woman caught in adultery, the Samaritan woman at the well, the hemorrhaging woman, the thieving tax collector. He understood that God's grace was evident in their lives. They were not sinners; they were children of God who had in some cases committed sins. But like the father of the prodigal son, Jesus never severed relationships. He showed that grace is present in every person, in every possibility.

Scripture teaches that grace is present in all of creation. Even with the presence of natural disasters and the dreadful evil perpetrated by some, the creation is not severed from God. Nowhere is this more beautifully stated than in the 139th Psalm:

Where can I go from your spirit?
   Or where can I flee from your presence?
If I ascend to heaven, you are there;
   If I make my bed in Sheol, you are there.
If I take the wings of the morning
   and settle at the farthest limits of the sea,
even there your hand shall lead me,
   and your right hand shall hold me fast.

The New Revised Standard Version subtitles the Psalm, "The Inescapable God." An equally apt title would be, "The God From Whom We Are Never Severed."

When we know and live this truth, it is impossible to classify people as outcasts, as inhuman. They, just as we, are part of God's creation, part of us, part of God. Any of us may strain the relationship, but it cannot be severed. That is what it means to be a child of God.

Wretches and Imprisonment

Just as in the days of slavery, many whites today still look upon people of color as essentially inferior — of a different order. Those differences of color are assumed to result in a fundamentally different kind of person. Even though many whites are out of work, many assume that unemployed blacks and Latinos are lazy and do not want to work. Though white marriages end in divorce almost 50% of the time, many see blacks and Latinos as uncommitted to family. Though half of the approximately 3000 inmates on death row nationally are white, many assume that black and Latino men have no regard for life. In each case, the negative behaviors of people of color are interpreted to be of a different order (not even just of a different magnitude) from the negative behaviors of white people.

When we take a close look at the penal system in our country, most especially the prisons, we discover an entire system based upon the classification of persons as wretches. The fact that a majority of the "wretches" are people of color is not an accident. It fits with the fundamental assumption of white racism that people of color are fundamentally inferior, prone to criminal behavior and lacking in responsibility. The classifications of people of color as inferior and of criminals as garbage to be thrown away have combined to foster a response to crime that is basically one of vengeance and punishment.

To create a response to crime that does not treat criminals as garbage but sees each as a child of God who is beautiful, worthwhile, and good in spite of crimes committed would be to create a revolution in our penal system. There are some who see the reality of grace present, even among criminals, and who have tried to respond accordingly. Later we will address such a possibility and investigate some of those attempts.

Of course the fact that all persons are God's children created in God's image does not mean that redemption is unnecessary. God's grace is a reality that all need to experience. This leads us to consider the question of redemption. Have we distorted it the same way we have distorted creation? Is the grace in redemption a grace that contributes to the spirit of vengeance and punishment or one that restores to wholeness?

CHAPTER THREE

| | |

Jesus and Me: The Individualization of Redemptive Grace

"Amazing grace, how sweet the sound, that saved a wretch like me. I once was lost, but now am found, was blind, but now I see." Perhaps John Newton penned the words in the first person singular for the sake of rhyme. "That saved some wretches like us" would be a difficult fit. But whatever the reason for his speaking of God's saving grace in individual terms, it certainly fits with Western Protestantism's distortion of redemptive grace.

Of course, it is absolutely true that redemption is experienced at the most deeply personal level. It is impossible to speak of redemption without acknowledging that fact. Our language offers us no option with which I am familiar that would recognize the personal nature of the experience without resorting to "me," "my," or "mine."

The problem is that in a society in which the isolated individual has been raised to the pinnacle of importance, first person singular words inevitably fail to signify the complexity and interrelatedness of all experience, even the most deeply personal. Protestantism has been seriously remiss in recognizing this truth. This is Protestantism's second serious limitation when it comes to understanding grace. Not only have we ignored or denied creation grace; we have individualized redemptive grace, thereby reinforcing the spirit of punishment.

Evangelistic meetings held in tents, convention centers, meeting halls, and churches were part of my youth growing up in fundamentalist Protestant Christianity. I was present at one of Billy Graham's first rallies, held on a riverboat steamer in Philadelphia in 1948. Local evangelists often stayed in our home while they were leading revivals at our congregation or the area Youth for Christ. Radio and television were inundated with Billy Graham clones who laid a mid-century version of Billy Sunday's sawdust trail across the nation. During this period, I responded to several altar calls and sat through innumerable others inviting persons to give their hearts to Jesus. I am grateful for the experience. Had it not been for those evangelistic meetings I may never have become a Christian or heard the call to ministry. These experiences indelibly shaped me during my formative years, teaching me that full life is to be found in giving more than in receiving. I was challenged to question the dominant values of the society around me and to be willing to stand up and be counted. I was taught about the fundamental mystery of God experienced in a world that seeks to reduce everything to numbers, commodities, and explanations. That formation has continued to shape me to this day.

There were also some tremendously injurious consequences for me, however, such as a biblicism that reduced would-be disciples to unquestioning adherents, a fixation on otherworldly matters to the exclusion of the material world, and extreme authoritarianism. Among the most destructive was the extreme, even exclusive, emphasis upon individual salvation — a matter strictly between God and me — which reinforced the already overwhelming sense I had picked up from the society around me that we are fundamentally isolated individuals. Even the constant exhortation to be concerned for others was largely limited to preaching to them so they could make an individual decision for Christ.

Chief among those whom we targeted for such outreach were the "bums" on skid row. The Sunday Breakfast Mission at the foot of the Benjamin Franklin Bridge in Philadelphia drew together men without homes, jobs, or hope. Most were alcoholics. While a meal and a bed were considered part of the mission's outreach, these were only instrumental to the "real" focus, which was the conversion of individuals. Never in my three years of service there did I hear anyone speak of the problem as anything other than individual men who were "down and out." There was no attention paid to what might have brought them to that point. Nor do I recall the sense among us that these men were flesh of my flesh and bone of my bone — brothers. They were simply objects of our pity and targets for our evangelism. At the Philadelphia Bible Institute, we kept count of how many of these individual souls we had won, much like the statistics of an NFL quarterback. We wore our "souls won to Christ" like notches on our belts or insignia on our helmets.

When I became a Presbyterian at age twenty-two, I assumed that the Presbyterian Church had a much broader view of evangelism. This was true, in part. My experience within so-called "mainline" Protestantism has generally been devoid of such crass headhunting. However, it seems to me that the basic sense of individualism has prevailed, albeit in a more "sophisticated" form. Despite all their social justice pronouncements and programs, when mainline Protestants speak of evangelism, their focus is generally on the individual's experience with God through Jesus Christ, leaving out any relationship to social structures and systems. This should come as no surprise, given what we know about the pervasiveness of individualism in our society. The churches are very much a part of their surrounding culture.[1]

The pervasiveness of individualism is often quite subtle. I was reminded of this several years ago while attending an ecumenical conference. Each of us introduced ourselves in the usual manner, offering the predictable information: name, job, place of residence, and occasionally family demographics, or some other personal tidbit. Then a Native American introduced himself — beginning four hundred years ago! He told of his ancestors and their migrations. It took fifteen minutes. It was quite apparent that he had a different concept

---

1. Robert Bellah et al., *Habits of the Heart: Individualism and Commitment in American Life* (Berkeley: University of California Press, 1985). Their extensive analysis of the individualism of American churches and society establishes this point quite substantially.

of "person" than most of the rest of us, for whom the isolated individual was the key. Our occasional references to family and community were more often than not afterthoughts, and when we did mention them it was not in relation to how they shaped us. They seemed to be appendages rather than integral elements of our personhood. It wasn't that we didn't love our families, only that we presented ourselves essentially as individuals first and only then as members of a family, neighborhood, or people. We assumed we could understand who we were apart from others, simply by reference to what we did and thought. For this Native American, the extended community was the key, with his own person emerging and understandable only within that context.

Individualism has been a hallmark of the United States since its inception as a nation of pioneers who left Europe for economic opportunity and religious freedom. Horace Greeley's exhortation "Go west, young man, go west" became the watchword of a society intent upon development at the expense of roots. Philip Slater has documented the cost of this constant push for new frontiers, which he called "the pursuit of loneliness."[2] Our continuing pursuit of loneliness continues in such modern creations as the portable CD or cassette players that make it possible to be in the midst of crowds of people yet oblivious to our surroundings, the single occupant automobiles that sit bumper to bumper in traffic jams, and the innumerable therapies that offer people a substitute for lack of community and intimate relationships. In each case, the isolation is fed by an affluence that enables us to purchase privacy through acquisition of material comforts. In the drive to make a place for ourselves as individuals, we have often cut ourselves off from the very connections that make us human. The increased emphasis upon the individual has led to narcissism and the destruction of community.

Unfortunately, this individualism has been reinforced by much of Protestant Christianity, not simply in its fundamentalist forms but

---

2. Philip Slater, *The Pursuit of Loneliness: American Culture at the Breaking Point,* rev. ed. (Boston: Beacon Press, 1976).

also within so-called mainline churches. Indeed, the longstanding division between evangelism and social witness within the various mainline denominations is evidence of how deep-seated this individualism is. It is common to hear the criticism that social witness, with its focus on structures, fails to deal with the more important issue of the care of the soul. There is an assumption of a hierarchy of importance: first the individual soul, then the larger corporate arena. At the core of popular Protestant Christianity is an understanding of redemptive grace that focuses upon the isolated individual.

Even a cursory look at the words of our hymns and our liturgical prayers reveals an emphasis upon individual guilt, individual forgiveness, individual holiness, and an individual relationship with God. Many of the prayers of confession focus upon the individual with little or no sense of corporate responsibility. One looks in vain for the corporate dimension of sin and redemption in one of the most common older confessions from the Reformed tradition still in frequent use today: "We have followed too much the devices and desires of our own hearts. We have offended against thy holy laws. We have left undone those things which we ought to have done; And we have done those things which we ought not to have done; And there is no health in us. But Thou, O Lord, have mercy upon us, miserable offenders."[3]

In the same manner, the assurance of pardon often reinforces the individualized nature of the forgiveness, received with primary reference to the individual heart and conscience. ". . . now fulfill in every contrite heart the promise of redeeming grace; remitting all our sins and cleansing us from an evil conscience . . . and keep us evermore in the peace and joy of a holy life. . . ."[4]

---

3. *The Book of Common Worship,* rev. ed. (Philadelphia: Presbyterian Board of Education, 1932), p. 5.

4. *Book of Common Worship,* p. 21.

Redemption as Corporate and Collective

To think solely, or even principally, in terms of individual sin and individual salvation is to distort reality. The Scriptures themselves, in which the strong sense of nation and collective is inescapable, challenge this distortion. Dorothee Sölle, in her critique of individualized notions of salvation, insists that, "Particularly in the Hebrew Bible, sin, like grace, is not primarily related to the individual but to the community, the people. . . ."[5]

Many others join her in this critique. The recovery of an understanding of the corporate, social, collective nature of sin and salvation has been at the heart of all recent liberation theologies. Latin American liberation theology has a highly developed notion of the sins of class-based economic structures, with attention paid to dependency theories, neo-colonialism, and exploitation. Black liberation theology emphasizes institutional as well as personal racism. Feminist liberation theologies have exposed the patriarchal assumptions and structures of sexism and heterosexism, and womanist theologies have shown us the linkages among racism, poverty, and patriarchy. Each of these movements has pointed to the collective nature of sin and salvation not only in terms of contemporary reality, but also in terms of the biblical witness. They each offer a hermeneutic that uncovers the collective meaning of the Scriptures. Each of these contemporary theologies shares the common realization that sin — and therefore saving grace — is corporate as well as personal, collective as well as individual.

Some would reject these approaches as fads. They are not fads; rather, they recover truth that has been alive in the church throughout its history, albeit a truth that often has been suppressed. During the nineteenth and early twentieth century, both in England and in the United States, the Social Gospel movement emphasized a corporate understanding of sin and grace. F. D. Maurice and Walter Rauschenbusch were the best-known proponents. Rauschenbusch

---

5. Dorothee Sölle, *Thinking About God: An Introduction to Theology* (Philadelphia: Trinity Press International, 1990), p. 77.

criticized what he saw as the church's accommodation to Pauline theology, especially influenced by the Reformation, and contrasted its emphasis upon individual salvation with what he understood as the heart of both prophetic Judaism and the ministry of Jesus. "The reign of God for which they [the prophets] hoped was therefore a social hope on fire with religion," according to Rauschenbusch. "Their concern was for the largest and noblest social group with which they were in contact — their nation."[6] He sees Jesus as a continuation of that major emphasis and suggests that it was the controlling notion for the people of Israel during Jesus' day, obviating the need for Jesus to explain what the Reign of God meant but leaving him free simply to announce its arrival:

> The Kingdom of God is the first and the most essential dogma of the Christian faith. It is also the lost social ideal of Christendom. No man is a Christian in the full senses of the original discipleship until he has made the Kingdom of God the controlling purpose of his life, and no man is intellectually prepared to understand Jesus Christ until he has understood the meaning of the Kingdom of God. The Reformation of the sixteenth century was a revival of Pauline theology. The present-day Reformation [meaning the Social Gospel movement] is a revival of the spirit and aims of Jesus himself.[7]

Earlier, during the time of the Reformation, we have the examples of Thomas Münzer, Andreas Karlstadt, and other radical reformers who understood that Satan was at work in the structures of church and state as well as within individuals. The movement of the Holy Spirit was leading the faithful into a battle against those structures. It was not simply a matter of persons needing to be changed but the society around them as well. Despite their emphasis upon the

6. Walter Rauschenbusch, *Christianizing the Social Order* (New York: Macmillan, 1921), p. 52.

7. Rauschenbusch, *Christianizing the Social Order,* p. 49.

personal witness of the Holy Spirit, they understood the implications of the Spirit in relation to the political life of their countries. Münzer called for the peasants to take up arms, and in his Sermon to the Princes of Saxony advised the princes with whom he sided that "a new Daniel must go forth . . . at the head of the troops. He must reconcile the anger of the princes and that of the enraged people. . . . Princes, they say, should do nothing but maintain civil order. Oh, beloved ones, the great stone will indeed soon fall on and smite this view of your office."[8]

John Calvin, who stands in the line of reformers challenging the monopolization of the means of grace in the hands of the Roman Catholic Church, understood this. While asserting the responsibility of each person before God, he also affirmed the responsibility of collective structures to participate in the redemptive process. Calvin viewed the spiritual and political as distinct and warned against a facile linkage. Nevertheless, he saw that the two orders, "while different . . . are not at variance."[9] Though he chose a more "establishment" approach than Thomas Münzer, who became a revolutionary, Calvin realized that institutions, including the state, could be instruments of God's redeeming grace. His experiment to set up a theocracy in Geneva in which the church provided guidance and structured leadership was an attempt to reflect faithfully the relationship between God's saving activity and the larger world. He believed that civil government played a crucial role in the Kingdom of God:

> Yet civil government has as its appointed end, so long as we live among men, to cherish and protect the outward worship of God, to defend sound doctrine of piety and the position of the church, to adjust our life to the society of men, to form our social behavior to civil righteousness, to reconcile us with one an-

8. Thomas Münzer, "Sermon to the Princes in the Radical Reformation," in *The Radical Reformation,* ed. Michael G. Baylor (Cambridge: Cambridge University Press, 1991), pp. 26-27.

9. John Calvin, *The Institutes of the Christian Religion,* Book IV, Chap. 20, trans. Ford Lewis Battles (Philadelphia: Westminster Press, 1960), p. 1486.

other, and to promote general peace and tranquility. All of this I admit to be superfluous, if God's Kingdom, such as it is now among us, wipes out the present life.[10]

In addition, Calvin gave great attention to the shape and governance of the church as Christ's visible body, while at the same time recognizing that the church was also invisible and not to be reduced simply to the visible form. In short, he considered institutions (church and state) as important as the soul.

This attention to corporate Christianity is reflected in the Scriptures as well. In the Hebrew Scriptures, the family (Abraham and Sarah, Isaac and Rebekah, and Jacob and Leah) and the nation are the contexts within which sin and redemption occur. Even the claim that the sins of the parents will be visited to the third and fourth generation points to the corporate nature of life.

When we move to the New Testament, the organic imagery of the body that fills the Pauline epistles leaves no doubt that we are absolutely interdependent. Ephesians 4 speaks of Christ as the head of the whole body, which, "joined and knit together by every ligament with which it is equipped, as each part is working properly, promotes the body's growth." The twelfth chapter of Hebrews refers to the "great cloud of witnesses" that surround believers. Hebrews 11 offers a litany of the saints who were counted righteous by God, who were part of the redemption going on in the world. They were both redeemed and redeeming — a dynamic in which both dimensions must remain inseparable. Verse 2 speaks of their personal redemption: "For by [their faith] the men of old received divine approval." Verse 33 speaks of their redeeming action in the society: they "through faith conquered kingdoms [and] enforced justice." Strikingly, that chapter ends with the recognition of the interconnectedness of believers through the ages. While the litany develops in a historical progression, building upon generation after generation, it ends by pointing to those who would come after: "All these, though

10. Calvin, *Institutes,* Book IV, Chap. XX, p. 1487.

well attested by their faith, did not receive what was promised, since God had foreseen something better for us, *that apart from us they should not be made perfect*" (vv. 39-40). In other words, not only do we draw upon the example, witness, and strength of this great cloud of witnesses who have gone before and figuratively cheer us on in the race, but the redemption of those giants of the faith is also somehow tied up with us as well. This collectivity is developed further in the words of Christ himself, who in Matthew 25 depicts not individuals being judged and cast out or received, but nations. Clearly the Bible illustrates a collective responsibility for which we are held accountable and a collective redemptive activity from which we all benefit.

In spite of its devotion to the words of the Bible, contemporary Protestantism has succumbed to the hyper-individualism of the culture. Drawing upon an essentially idealist philosophical tradition that has come down through much of post-Augustinian orthodoxy, the Reformation, and neo-orthodoxy, it has failed to understand the strong communal strain within its own history and, most fundamentally, within Scripture. Voices in both Protestant history and the Bible reject the flight to individualism and set forth an understanding of redemption as corporate, political, and communal, while at the same time deeply personal. Redemptive grace operates in community, through community, and for community. Each person's redemption is inextricably linked with the redemption and redemptive activity of the community.

Lest I be misunderstood, let me underscore that I am not suggesting an abdication of personal responsibility or a denial of personal redemption. None of this takes away from our responsibility in daily deciding the course of our lives, the voices to which we respond, and the values we prize. We bear full responsibility for our choices and will be held accountable for them. Nor does it imply that the transformation that redemption generates is less than fully personal. Our very orientation, motivations, and values — all core elements of our personhood — are subject to transforming grace. But we are always set within the context of our collective, communal reality, which also will be held accountable and which also needs redeeming. We must not neglect one for the other, because our neglect of the corporate, collective dimensions and aspects of redemption has led to some very serious consequences.

Individualized Redemption and the Denial of Complicity

When the Bible speaks of the sins of the parents being visited to the third and fourth generations, it recognizes a truth that has been largely ignored in Western church and society. Sin is infectious and spreads like an epidemic. It has to do not only with a person's choice, but also with a person's context. Placing all responsibility for sin upon the individual is a convenient denial of the larger community's complicity — its choices, policies, and structures. Such one-sided assignment of guilt is similar to blaming the person who contracts a potent communicable disease for not washing hands or keeping a healthy distance. It may well be that such behavior contributed to contracting the disease, but if the disease had not been present in the society, the behavior would not have found anything to spread. Both elements — personal and social — are involved. I was struck by the words of James Irwin, who had worked for twenty-six years at the Maine Youth Center. Responding to the public's outcry over rising youth violence, he registered puzzlement at the public's surprise, adding that he had never met a murderer whose behavior couldn't be explained by the murderer's childhood experiences.[11]

There are social as well as individual factors that contribute to aberrant behavior. Perhaps such truisms need not be repeated here, but I suspect that they must. For in adopting a notion of redemptive grace that is individualized, we have inadvertently accepted its corollary, that the problem of sin is individualized. The Dalai Lama, responding to a question about his anger at the 1990 Gulf War, painted a picture of the circle of complicity involved:

11. "The Violent Society Reaches Maine," *Maine Times,* November 12, 1993.

. . . when people started blaming Saddam Hussein, then my heart went out to him . . . because this blaming everything on him — it's unfair. He may be a bad man, but without his army, he cannot act as aggressively as he does. And his army, without weapons, cannot do anything. And these weapons were not produced in Iraq itself. Who supplied them? Western nations! So one day something happened and they blamed everything on him — without acknowledging their own contributions. That's wrong.[12]

To think of redemption — and therefore sin — in individualized terms allows us to deny our complicity in the matter. But we cannot wash our hands of our collective responsibility. That is the significance of the notion of the fall, or of the claim that in Adam all die. It is not necessary to believe in the fall as having ontologically corrupted every human born in order to recognize the pervasiveness and power of sin at work in all social relationships and social structures. We do not enter the world as individuals with a blank slate. We are born into a context that is filled with sin. Sin is a corporate, collective reality as well as a personal one; so too is redemption. It is important when we think of redemptive grace that we avoid an individualized concept of sin and salvation, or we will easily fall into the trap of assigning the responsibility for sin too narrowly.

Herein lies one of the most significant failures of our criminal justice system. It seldom recognizes the enslavement of the criminal to a criminal community, drugs, hopelessness, and the culture of crime. It treats perpetrators as if their actions were totally self-contained. One exception to this myopia is the increasing recognition of the abusive context that has led some women to violent behavior, including murder; increasingly, our society is coming to understand that these women have been enslaved by abusive spouses and acted out of desperation and fear. For the most part, however, our penal system exhibits inadequate realization of the need for a re-

12. "The Dalai Lama," *The New York Times Magazine*, Nov. 28, 1993, p. 54.

demptive process that goes beyond a focus on the one committing the crime.

It strikes me as strange that a theology that has made so much of the sacrificial death of Christ on our behalf should have such difficulty finding room for a response to crime that involves more than just the criminal. The idea of the first and second Adam as representatives points to the collective, connected nature of all human experience, whether in terms of sin or redemption. Unfortunately, in western culture, which bifurcates reality — individual versus collective, spiritual versus material — the representativeness of Adam and Jesus has been understood in metaphysical terms. The result has been that the historical, material connection between Adam and us and between Jesus and us has been lost.

But a metaphysical explanation of representativeness is not the only possible one, nor is it even the most appropriate one, given the mindset of Israel and the primitive church. They lived in a culture that understood itself in a collective sense. Adam's act had its impact upon all of us — in Adam, all have sinned. Jesus' life and ministry had a collective impact — in him, all are made alive. The impact is because of our connectedness, not because of some metaphysical transaction.

It is important to recognize that the biblical writers described the reality that they, in their community, experienced. Theirs was not a speculative metaphysic but a poetic, cosmological description of what was happening to them. The difference between a speculative metaphysical explanation and an experiential cosmological one is evident when we talk about our own relationships today. To explain my relationship to my wife as ordained by God or willed in heaven is to acknowledge its depths and dimensions with a language that cannot be circumscribed. It is to lodge it within the deepest mysteries of the universe. To think that this translates into an explanation for how we met, implying control or influence that somehow comes from beyond history, is simply speculation.

Because of these different linguistic contexts, to speculate about the mystery of sin or redemption is absurd. We do not know how sin occurred or how it spreads. Even those who entertain contemporary scientific explanations find themselves at odds. Is it nurture or nature? Two persons (perhaps even siblings) born and raised in similarly oppressive circumstances turn out entirely different. One commits murder and is imprisoned. The other becomes a social worker with the homeless. What caused the difference? Was it the genes? Was it their place in the sibling hierarchy? Was it God's will? Was it the socialization of parents, schools, and peers? Was it some outside intervention? Was it the individual choices each made? We do not know why each took the path they took. In the same way, we do not know how the life and death of Jesus fit within the great drama of redemption. To speak of Adam's sin as bringing death and Jesus' obedience bringing justification (Romans 5) describes what Paul and others experienced. To turn these words into a metaphysical explanation about a transaction that takes place above and beyond history is to fall into a mode of understanding foreign to Israel and most of the primitive church.

We are all connected. That is the truth of Jesus' claim that he did not come to abolish the law but to fulfill it. Jesus recognized that it was impossible not to stand within his tradition, even the one against which he was constantly struggling. By drawing a division between law and gospel, Jesus and Moses, or Adam and Jesus, we do a fundamental disservice to Jesus' and the early church's understanding of the connectedness of all things.

This is not meant to deny personal accountability. It is clear in Scripture that we are each held responsible for our decisions and actions. Jesus unhesitatingly called lies, greed, vengeance, and self-righteousness for what they are. He, along with Paul, Nathan, Moses, and others, recognized that there are dire consequences to our sin — even separation and death.

Protestants haven't had a problem holding individuals accountable. That has been our strong suit. We have long recognized that each of us bears responsibility for our choices and actions. The problem for Western Christianity has been in moving beyond our severe individualism to a corporate sense of sin and redemption. According to Dorothee Sölle,

Such ritualistic conceptions [sacrificial offering] have no roots in our culture. For us, the person, understood as the individual, is responsible for his or her actions. There is no one else who could intervene. Just as each person dies for himself or herself, so also each individual is responsible for himself or herself. For this way of thinking, the concept of grace remains irregular and absurd.[13]

As Sölle suggests, our problem has been the failure to understand the collective or social nature of sin and redemption. This failure has numerous consequences. First, failure to understand the corporate nature of sin and redemption can lead to inappropriate guilt. If everything finally comes down to our choices and actions, then we must bear full responsibility and, hence, guilt for what we do and its consequences. Of course, guilt is often an appropriate and healthy response. My failure to act lovingly to someone in need and their consequent harm — when I had the time, resources, and opportunity — is something for which I rightly should feel guilt and be held accountable. On the other hand, there is sometimes an inappropriate sense of guilt — guilt for things beyond our control, such as the guilt some children feel when their parents divorce or the guilt sometimes felt by someone brutalized by rape. One of the problems with carrying this inappropriate guilt is that we become overloaded and immobilized, unable then to deal with even appropriate guilt with respect to other matters.

Simplifying responsibility and guilt by thinking only in terms of individuals also enables those who participate in systems or structures of evil to deny their complicity and guilt. For example, parties who sue for divorce often speak as if only the other were to blame, failing to recognize how they themselves participated in the creation of a failing relationship.

This is especially true when it comes to many forms of crime. Society often acts as if the criminal act were committed in a vacuum,

13. Sölle, *Thinking About God,* p. 83.

as if the person committing the crime were simply making a choice. But on every occasion the choice is made in a context that often sets limits and exerts pressure. In *Sophie's Choice,* a Jewish mother is given the "choice" by a Nazi officer to save either her daughter or her son from the gas chamber, but not both. Her decision haunts her every day the rest of her life, making it impossible for her to find healthy relationships. Her feelings of guilt have overtaken her. No one seeing the film or reading that novel can possibly fail to recognize the coercion under which she acted and the tragic self-destructiveness of her guilt.

The forces at work upon Sophie are different only in their stark clarity, but not in kind, from the forces at work in so many situations of crime. A young man joins a gang and is involved in a fight and a killing. Behind that act often are layers of forces that move him toward that terrible moment: a broken family, failure at school, hopelessness within his community, a lack of self-esteem, and severe poverty. Seeking family, he turns to the gang. Seeking self-esteem, he acts tough. Seeking money, he turns to dealing. Seeking approval, he kills.

Intermingled with those layers of forces that move him toward his decision are other layers, often hidden and usually denied: the forces of racism that permit certain communities to languish in poverty by failing to invest in them or to provide adequate educational resources; the forces of a market economy that allow workers to be downsized and businesses closed for the sake of the bottom line. At the same time, many of us who are economically privileged benefit from these arrangements. Our children go to schools with first-class resources, and our investments increase. But when it comes to deciding who is guilty for the murder, many believe that the only consideration is the "choice" of that young man.

We treat certain persons who commit crimes as if they alone were responsible, and as if they alone must be punished or rehabilitated. But the truth of the matter is that crime is a collective problem. According to a 1992 report in the *New York Times,* "75 percent of the [New York] state's entire prison population comes from just seven neighborhoods in New York City." The report focused on the work of

Eddie Ellis, released after twenty-three years in prison. During that time, he has become one of the state's leading unaccredited penologists, first from within the prison, and now on the streets. He calls these seven neighborhoods "symbiotic neighborhoods." "'In our analysis,' Ellis said, 'we found out in detail how symbiotic it is, how prison is heavily influenced by inner-city underclass subculture in just a few neighborhoods. It's a direct relationship, an umbilical cord.'"[14]

Eric Staub, in a brilliant analysis of the roots of evil,[15] traces a number of factors that led up to four of the major historic genocides of the 20th century: the Holocaust, Cambodia, Armenia, and Argentina. In each case, one of the significant factors was the complicity of bystanders who either lent their support to developments or were passive in the face of the rising horror. One of the most troubling questions each of us must ask ourselves is the extent to which we are complicit in the creation and sustaining of these seven neighborhoods and others like them — in the creation and sustaining of the symbiosis. The symbiosis is larger than simply that between the seven neighborhoods and those who commit crimes. The symbiosis extends to the larger society and the condition of those seven neighborhoods.

When we lose sight of the umbilical connection between criminal acts and the larger social collectivity, it is a simple step to deal with crime by dealing with the criminal as an isolate — a simple but tragic step. In so doing we make true redemption impossible, for redemption must include all within the scope of the symbiosis. To omit reference to the symbiotic neighborhoods, the larger circles of complicity, or to the victims of the crime is to render any possibility of redemption moot, even in those cases where dealing with the criminal is expressly intended to rehabilitate. Since most prisoners upon release return to the neighborhoods from which they came (95 percent by some estimates),[16] it is not surprising that more than 50 per-

14. *New York Times,* Dec. 23, 1992.
15. Eric Staub, *The Roots of Evil: The Origins of Genocide and Other Group Violence* (Cambridge: Cambridge University Press, 1997).
16. *New York Times,* Dec. 23, 1992.

cent return to prison. Recidivism is a predictable result when we deal with crime as an individual's problem rather than as a collective reality demanding a more holistic redemption. Seeking justice by singling out perpetrators as *the* problem guarantees that, like Sisyphus, we will continuously have to roll the same stone up the same hill over and over again; at the end of the day, we will have gotten nowhere. Perhaps one day the stone itself will finally overcome us.

Hand in hand with the individualizing of redemptive grace is its dehistoricization. Much of Western Christianity has reduced the ongoing struggle for redemption to a once-for-all event that has been accomplished by God. There is nothing more to be done but to acknowledge and receive it. Karl Barth has reinforced this notion of a battle having been fought and won beyond the plains of history, one that places us in an interim time:

> In the Resurrection of Jesus Christ the claim is made that God's victory, in the person of his Son, has already been won. Easter is indeed the great pledge of our hope, but simultaneously this future is already present in the Easter message. It is the proclamation of a victory already won. The war is at an end. . . . The game is won, even though the player can still play a few further moves. . . . It is in this interim space that we are living, the old is past, behold it has all become new.[17]

The problem is that this notion easily contributes to passivity in the historical arena. If this time is merely interim, we need only wait for the final consummation of history, which God has already guaranteed. At a fundamental level, nothing we do can finally make a difference, except to bring others to this knowledge. We are easily reduced to individualizing once again.

The redemption demanded by the cosmic evil that threatens our world must itself be cosmic. In the face of radical evil, nothing less than an all-encompassing grace will do. That is the truth behind the

17. Karl Barth, *Dogmatics in Outline* (London: SCM Press, 1958), p. 122.

metaphor that God had to give his own Son in order for redemption to occur. It was an act of grace without reservation, without limits.

Thinking of redemption grace in individualistic terms denies the fullness of what we are up against, and at the same time it denies the fullness of God's grace. Further, it allows us to escape our responsibility for redemptive activity in the face of crime and to blame the perpetrators. Fortunately, there are some who have glimpsed a broader vision of what must be done, who have understood redemption as involving all of the actors and systems in the human dilemma, offering an alternative to the punitive spirit that has captured our nation.

| | |

CHAPTER FOUR

Is There Anything Else Out There?
Restorative Justice Alternatives

When I first began thinking about issues of criminal justice, I had imagined that the problem was a lack of effective, humane, and beneficial alternatives. I was wrong. Alternatives that contribute to the health and healing of criminals, victims, and the larger society are currently in use around the world and have been available for centuries. The primary problem is not an absence of viable alternatives to our current punitive response, but rather a problem of knowledge and of will. The average citizen is unaware of the alternatives, in large measure due to the systematic refusal on the part of those in control to inform them. As a consequence, there seems to be no alternative but to punish. Given the fear and anger that average citizens harbor, their punitive response is both understandable and predictable. The tragedy is that many in power who do know of the alternatives have chosen to ignore them and instead to pander to the fears and prejudices of the masses. Ignoring all the evidence that something better is available, they operate instead out of their desire to get even, and in so doing contribute to a broader spirit of punishment.

One of the most hopeful developments in the past few decades is the growing interest in restorative justice. Its roots lie in many ancient cultures and its current expressions can be found in penal practices throughout the world. Politicians and the media have lulled many people into thinking that there is only one way to deal with criminals effectively: "lock them up and throw away the key." There is at least a chance that broader knowledge about restorative alternatives will make it more difficult for the punitive spirit to continue unabated.

Even though responses to crime have varied widely throughout history, most of us are familiar only with the retributive approach. Retributive justice is essentially a punitive response focused on paying back for harm done. It has taken the forms of imprisonment, public humiliation (as in the use of stockades), fines, servitude, solitary isolation, sensory deprivation, chemical and physical alteration, exile, physical and psychological punishment, and death. In the retributive response, the victim and the community are only abstractly involved, while the primary focus is upon the perpetrator. In Western jurisprudence, the injured party is assumed to be the state, which then stands as a representative of the victim.

The notion that crime is essentially an offense against the state is a rather recent development, having its roots in the late medieval claim of the king that criminal acts disturbed the king's peace. Treating the state (or the king) as the injured party strengthened the control of the state. Crimes were defined as those acts that broke the law, rather than as those that violated the relationship between the offender and victim or members of the community. Punishment for lawbreaking, then, rather than actions taken to restore damaged relationships and injured parties, became the operative orientation. Getting well took a back seat to getting even.

There is, however, a longstanding tradition of restorative justice, not as well known as the retributive response, and with significantly different purposes and characteristics. Restorative justice, according to Daniel Van Ness, brings "victims, offenders and the community together with government in repairing injuries caused by crime."[1]

---

1. Daniel W. Van Ness, "Restorative Justice and International Human Rights," in *Restorative Justice: International Perspectives,* ed. Burt Galaway and Joe Hudson (Monsey, NY: Criminal Justice Press, 1996), p. 9.

This brand of justice emphasizes repairing all the injured parties, including victims, offenders, and the community. They understand that all the relationships among the parties implicated in the circle of crime are in need of healing and restoration. While the levels and forms of injury to victims, perpetrators, and the larger community differ, the intent of restorative justice is to attend to all three. Thus the restorative approach expands its focus far beyond retribution.

Restorative justice is based on three fundamental assumptions:

1. Crime is primarily a conflict between individuals, resulting in injuries to victims, communities, and the offenders themselves; only secondarily is it the breaking of law.
2. The overarching aim of the criminal justice process should be to reconcile parties while repairing the injuries caused by crime.
3. The criminal justice process should facilitate active participation by victims, offenders, and their communities. It should not be dominated by the government to the exclusion of others.[2]

The differences between retributive and restorative justice are striking. Retributive justice is primarily concerned with maintaining power, while restorative justice is concerned with restoring relationships. Retributive justice is primarily concerned with punishment, while restorative justice is concerned with healing. Retributive justice focuses on a narrowly circumscribed set of actors — the offender and the state — while restorative justice seeks to encompass the larger circle of injury and destruction that includes the victims and the community. Retributive justice utilizes punishment as its primary approach, while restorative justice utilizes mediation, non-punitive sanctions, reparations, and the full participation of all those damaged.

There are a number of contemporary models of restorative justice, none of which encompasses the entirety of possible restorative methods, but when taken together, constitute an impressive picture

2. Van Ness, "Restorative Justice," p. 259.

of what is possible when retribution gives way to restoration. These include but are not limited to: the South African Truth and Reconciliation Commission, Sweden's criminal justice system, New Zealand's juvenile justice approach, Native American sentencing circles, and some restorative alternatives already at work in the American system, including the victim-offender reconciliation process in Minnesota. While there are many other possibilities to consider, these are a powerful witness to the possibility of healing rather than retribution.

The Truth and Reconciliation Commission in South Africa

For more than one hundred years, South Africa's racist policies and practices were infamous. With the advent of apartheid in 1948, racism was codified in a formal manner, with its attendant hierarchy of power and privilege: the white Afrikaners at the top, descending to Indians, coloreds (people of mixed race), and finally blacks. Treatment of the non-Afrikaners varied according to groups, including passes required for blacks (similar to passports) to move between areas within the country; random arrest and torture; enforced resettlement of huge populations to unplanned townships that generally lacked infrastructure, water, sewerage, and public services; discriminatory hiring practices and pay patterns; and two-tiered educational and healthcare systems.

In response to the inhumanity of apartheid, people across the racial and political spectrum spoke out, organized, and resisted. Armed struggle became common as a means to seek change. While not all sympathizers supported the armed struggle advocated by the African National Congress (ANC), a growing international movement of solidarity developed that eventually came to include some of the boardrooms of corporate capitalism. Media attention, economic sanctions, protests, and fundraising came from throughout the world.

In the early 1990s, in one of the most dramatic reversals in history, South Africa dismantled this oppressive system, and blacks gained political control with the first fully free elections since the beginning of apartheid. During the 1994 elections people turned out to vote in unexpected numbers, despite disruptions and threats of violence. The result of the election was an overwhelming ANC majority in the legislature and the choice of Nelson Mandela as the nation's first black president.

The interim constitution of 1993 offered amnesty for political crimes committed during the years 1960-1993 of the apartheid era, and it was an important step in the dismantling of apartheid. With Mandela's election to office, the ruling party struggled with whether to honor the promise of amnesty. Many new leaders had suffered greatly, Mandela himself having spent twenty-seven years in prison. Bitterness was inevitable and the temptation for vengeance was understandable. Some called for Nuremberg-like trials, seeking vengeance against those responsible for the atrocities of apartheid. But the ANC majority and other members of the parliament believed that national healing was more crucial than getting even and decided to honor the interim constitution's pledge of amnesty. Amnesty alone, however, could not lead to national healing; that would simply allow the perpetrators of political crimes during apartheid to escape responsibility for their actions. Amnesty, as incorporated in the 1993 interim constitution, was designed primarily as a protection for the white perpetrators of apartheid. The new government, under Mandela's strong leadership, understood that national healing demanded a broader process. Simply granting amnesty to the former oppressors was certain to result in cries of outrage and a sense of betrayal among the victims and their families.

Out of this concern arose the Truth and Reconciliation Commission (TRC), which was given as its mandate three broad tasks:

1. To lift up before the world, by soliciting the truth from both victims and perpetrators, the painful narrative of the gross violations of human rights that occurred during apartheid.

2. To grant amnesty (under certain conditions) for crimes and atrocities committed with political intent, pursuant to full disclosure by the perpetrators.
3. To seek means for rehabilitation of the victims and the larger society through such avenues as reparations, face-to-face encounters, and dignified treatment of victims and their families.

The TRC process has been extraordinary by almost any measure. While it is not without its critics — some severe — it has shown the nation and the world a way in which crimes can be addressed in a manner that affords dignity and healing to all involved. In case after case, families of victims have met face to face with those who tortured or killed their loved ones. Their stories have filled the newspapers, radio, and television. No longer can people claim ignorance; no longer is the suffering hidden and silent. The pain of those encounters often has been overwhelming, bringing even the commissioners to tears. While not all the perpetrators have expressed regret or remorse, many have. Sometimes the families of the victims have found it within their hearts to offer forgiveness and to embrace the ones who killed their kin. Those are powerful moments.

I spent several hours in a home in Gugulatu, a black township outside Cape Town. In that modest home three mothers who had collectively had five children killed told their story. They had appeared before the TRC and had expressed their willingness to forgive the killers and move on with their lives. They spoke to me of their grief, acknowledged their continuing bitterness, and complained that the meager reparations they were receiving from the government did not meet the costs of raising their grandchildren, for whom they were now the guardians. When I asked how it was possible for them to forgive the perpetrators, one said she was not sure that she could, at least not yet. The others indicated that they could not live with harboring the bitterness and anger any longer; for their own peace, forgiveness was necessary. Each of them stated that for the sake of building a new society for their grandchildren, the cycle of vengeance needed to be broken by forgiveness.

The TRC is not a perfect process by any means. Some believe that the perpetrators are getting off too easily. They have criticized the process as offering "cheap reconciliation" which does not demand remorse, repentance, or reparations from the perpetrators — simply acknowledgment of their deeds in exchange for amnesty. Steven Biko's family has refused to honor the process. In addition, the modest reparations that occasionally have been made available to victims have come largely from extremely limited government sources. Regrettably, many of those Afrikaners who benefited financially from apartheid have resisted calls for a reparation tax. There is a glimmer of hope, however: several nations have begun to consider a reparations fund to begin the process of redressing the injustice of the old system. Norway and Sweden have already contributed to such a fund.

The criticisms of the TRC, however, must be balanced by a consideration of its successes to date, as well as the alternatives. Charles Villa-Vicencio has underscored the necessary compromises that must be made in the political arena and recognizes the TRC as a step in this direction. Quoting Justice Richard Goldstone, he defends the compromise as the best option: "The decision to opt for a TRC was an important compromise. If the ANC had insisted on Nuremberg-style trials for the leaders of the former apartheid government, there would have been no peaceful transition to democracy, and if the former government had insisted on a blanket amnesty, then, similarly, the negotiations would have broken down. A bloody revolution sooner rather than later would have been inevitable. The TRC is a bridge from the old to the new."[3] Further, of the 2370 cases reviewed by the commission as of February 1998, 2234 were tossed out "because the applicants — many scheming to get out of prison — could not show a political motive for their crimes. The Commission has heard about 100 of the remaining cases, with sixty receiving amnesty

3. Charles Villa-Vicencio, "From Coexistence to Reconciliation; The TRC: A Step Along the Way" (paper presented at a conference on "The Possibilities of Memory and Justice: The Holocaust and Apartheid," Yale University, February 8-9, 1998), p. 2.

and forty-three denied it because the Commission did not believe they were telling the truth."[4]

The TRC is not perfect, but it is a serious step toward a process of healing that is not based upon recrimination, vengeance, and violence. One observer, L. Gregory Jones, finds the commission "one of the most dramatic and hopeful signs of an authentically Christian contribution to political life to emerge in many years."[5] The TRC process is shaped, of course, by a much wider set of assumptions and factors than simply those of the Christian tradition, so it may not be fully appropriate to label this a "Christian" contribution. Among them is the Ubuntu philosophy of Africa, which affirms the essential connection of all living things. Another influence on the shape of the TRC process that does not come out of the Christian tradition is the 1993 agreement on amnesty for the former apartheid criminals, arranged by the criminals themselves. Nonetheless, many of the TRC's architects and participants — Archbishop Desmond Tutu being the most prominent — do draw upon their Christian faith as the foundation for this approach. It is certainly fair to say that the TRC is significantly shaped by and in line with some central emphases of the Christian faith.

The consequences of the TRC process often have been both dramatic and healing. When perpetrators and victims can find themselves embracing forgiveness and treating each other as persons of dignity and worth; when reparations can be made, however imperfect, to those who have suffered loss; when people who lived in denial can now acknowledge the truth about their culture; and when evil is exposed, surely healing has begun.

The TRC alone, of course, cannot bring about healing. Without economic justice, the entire basis for national healing will dissolve. While political control has shifted from whites to people of color, economic control has not. There is a growing black and colored middle class, but ownership of the natural resources, media, communica-

---

4. Zia Jaffrey, "Desmond Tutu," *The Progressive,* Feb. 18, 1998.
5. "How Much Truth Can We Take?" *Christianity Today,* Feb. 9, 1998, p. 22.

tions companies, financial houses, and other major businesses and industries remains largely in white control. The gap between whites and people of color remains significant, and entire portions of the population — primarily those residing in the townships — are suffering from severe unemployment and underemployment. Despair and crime are increasing in the townships as the people wait, seemingly in vain, for a better day. A joke making the rounds in the Cape Flats, a devastatingly poor township outside Cape Town, explained the rising crime rate this way: America has Bob Hope, Johnny Cash, and Stevie Wonder, while the Cape Flats has no hope, no cash, and so no wonder. The hopes of the people for a better life under the new government largely have been thwarted. Despairing of a better life, tens of thousands of young people have joined gangs that in many locations are beyond police control. They exist and roam at will, creating one of the most dangerous countries in the world. It is estimated that there are 80,000 gang members in the Cape Flats alone. Cape Town is now known as the murder capital of the world. Kidnappings are common in the cities, and in some areas around Johannesburg carjackings are an everyday occurrence, sometimes involving the murder of the occupants.

This dramatic onslaught of crime and terrorism has given rise to calls for tougher police action, more severe penalties, and the building of more prisons. It is tragic and ironic that in a nation whose TRC is a model of healing and reconciliation for the world the cries for vengeance toward common street crime are increasing. Voices from every quarter are calling for the restoration of the death penalty. Pleas for reconciliation and symbolic acts of forgiveness will not silence these cries. Only when economic justice is joined with political justice will healing be possible. Healing is a circular process, and all dimensions of the circle must be attended to in order for healing to occur. The TRC process will have to be accompanied by more significant reparations, so that lives and communities can be rebuilt. There is a separate commission for reparations that is seeking to address the larger circle of healing, but its resources are quite limited, and it has received less attention than the TRC process.

Despite the insufficient level of economic redress, however, the TRC process has become a remarkable beacon of hope in the midst of a vengeful world, reaching even into the prisons of South Africa. The Pulmor Prison in Cape Town is one of the largest in South Africa, and had for many years been notorious for its inhumane treatment. A group of prisoners met with me for several hours in the library, where they shared their histories, their crimes, their conversions, and their experience in prison. All but one acknowledged their guilt and the legitimacy of their sentence, and the one exception was in the process of an appeal. All of them spoke of the humaneness of the treatment they were receiving, and those who had been imprisoned for longer terms mentioned the changes that had occurred since the end of apartheid. While all longed for release, none spoke of mistreatment, or of being demeaned. We closed with a time of prayer, which was led, at the prisoners' request, by their "brother" the guard.

From the minister of justice, to the prison wardens, to the guards, I was struck by the impact that the notion of reconciliation and healing is having upon the treatment of those who commit crimes. It is not just the past that is being transformed by the TRC process, but the present and future as well. If it is possible for those who have suffered the loss of dignity, freedom, quality of life, and loved ones to forgive and seek to rebuild their society, do they not offer an important challenge to our spirit of punishment?

Criminal Justice in Sweden

Shortly after my trip to South Africa, I spent time in Sweden, a nation that is dramatically different from South Africa in many respects. It is a significantly wealthy, homogeneous nation, shaped by Nordic and Christian heritages, with an economy that is a modified form of democratic socialism. Economic disparities are not severe, abject poverty is virtually unknown, and human rights have been honored to an unusual degree.

Sweden's approach to criminal justice has been to avoid punishment and prison whenever possible. The Swedish government assumes that it cannot prepare people for responsible participation in community by removing them from the community. It uses other sanctions and remedies such as probation, counseling, electronic bracelets, and community service, all with the aim of rehabilitation. There are less than 4000 people in prison out of a population of more than 8.5 million. The rate of imprisonment in the United States is more than fifteen times that of Sweden.

There are many reasons for the difference in rate of imprisonment between Sweden and the United States, but none more important than homogeneity. The more homogeneous the group, the less likely it is to respond punitively. Even in Sweden, increasing heterogeneity through immigration from Eastern Europe and the Middle East has led to noticeable changes in the policies, practices, and spirit of the nation. While the overall rate of imprisonment has not risen appreciably, in the ten years between 1987 and 1997 there have been fewer and fewer pardons given from long sentences, the definition of a lifetime sentence has gone from ten to eighteen years, and there has been an increase in longer-term sentences (five years or more).

The spirit of the culture is changing as well. Increasing numbers of young people are calling for the death penalty and other tougher measures. There is evidence of racism and ethnocentrism in the number of immigrants imprisoned relative to their percentage of the population. The cry for getting tougher has paralleled the increasing number of immigrants. At a certain level this is understandable, since by all accounts immigrants are conducting most of the drug trafficking. It is interesting to note that the cries for getting tough are not coming from the politicians, as is the case in our nation, but rather from the younger generation. In conversation, some chaplains and justice system officials attributed the rise of a punitive spirit among the young people to the influence of U.S. television and movies.

Still, Sweden's approach continues to emphasize rehabilitation and avoiding recidivism. A majority connected with the penal system know that the longer the imprisonment, the greater the chances for recidivism. One chaplain indicated that there is an inverse proportion between length of imprisonment and recidivism: 24% recidivism for those not imprisoned, 52% for those imprisoned from one to two years, and 86% for those imprisoned more than ten years.

Even when the Swedish system deems imprisonment appropriate, its treatment is in stark contrast to what occurs in most prisons within the United States. In the United States the wave of the future is longer terms, harsher treatment and sensory deprivation cells, in which prisoners are denied human contact (even visual). In Sweden, the emphasis is upon respect and rehabilitation. At one maximum-security prison in Norrköping, five young men had a suite of rooms, including a common kitchen, dining area, and living room, and each had his own bedroom with a door that closed. Each bedroom had a desk, a television set, bookshelves, pictures, and curtains. While not luxurious by any means, the accommodations were pleasant.

The guards and prisoners I observed interacted warmly and comfortably. A female guard was working with two of the men, training them how to bake breads. At one point she put her hand on a prisoner's shoulder while she talked with him. Another prisoner was being privately tutored in math. A tutor comes three days a week for several hours at a time to work with three of the young men who have not completed high school. All guards in Sweden undergo at least one year of special training following graduation from high school. Many have received additional training, and it shows in the care and professionalism with which they carry out their work. One regional director of prisons spoke of the need for those working with prisoners to be as giraffes: with big hearts that generate respect and long necks that can look behind and see the pain.

One young man of twenty proudly showed my wife his room and began to talk about his life, his family, and his future. He was from Turkey, had been in prison for about eighteen months, and saw no immediate chance for release. He did not seem bitter, but grateful for the treatment he was receiving. He told me he had expected to be treated far worse than he was; surprisingly, he felt respected as a human being. I later found out that he had been convicted of murder.

The prison chaplains, with whom I spent several days, serve not as a buffer between the privileged and the oppressed, but as active supporters of rehabilitation and community healing. They see their roles as advocates for the prisoners as well as pastors to both them and the guards. They play an increasingly important role in linking parishes with prisons, prisoners, and those released. In the past seven years, the number of chaplains has increased from ten to forty, and they gather regularly under the auspices of the Swedish Christian Council for theological reflection, networking, and planning. Besides the chaplains, there are almost two hundred clergy involved in committee and pastoral work related to prisoners. It is common to find parish groups, prison chaplains, theological faculty, and current and former prisoners interacting.

The interchange among clergy, former inmates, inmates, and chaplains struck me during several seminars I attended. There was clearly a fundamental mutual respect. Later I read a description of the goal of pastoral care in the prisons in a newsletter published by the Swedish Christian Council in March 1994. It clarifies the foundation on which they build:

> Pastoral care within the prison service aims to give the inmates back their self-esteem, strengthen their motivation and help them to face life again. This is achieved mainly by means of personal contact guided by Christian ethics.
>
> In simple terms these fundamental precepts can be expressed as follows:
> - all people have equal value and dignity irrespective of their actions
> - all people have their own resources for positive development.[6]

While it would be foolish to try to draw too many conclusions from such brief contact, it appears that there is a level of decency at

6. "Corrections in Sweden," newsletter of the Swedish Christian Council, March 1994, p. 2.

work in the Swedish criminal justice system that provides significant resources for restoration. One former prisoner spoke of finding grace in prison, though he didn't fully recognize it at the time. Many regarded prison as a place of grace, forgiveness, and healing rather than punishment. One chaplain summed it up well: "It is impossible to be a prison chaplain and not think this way theologically."

New Zealand's Youth Court

After the United States, New Zealand has more persons imprisoned than any other Western nation (though we imprison four times as many as New Zealand, making us by far the "winner" in the race to get tough on crime). Despite a steady increase in the prison population in New Zealand over the last twenty years, crime has also increased, leading some to conclude that non-punitive alternatives must be found.

In 1989, the government passed the *Children, Young Persons and Their Families Act,* an extraordinary measure by most accounts. This is a genuinely new paradigm for dealing with youth offenders and is based on a restorative concept of justice. Judge F. W. M. McElrea, Youth Court liaison judge for Auckland, suggests that there are three radical changes involved in this new process: "the transfer of power from the state to the community, the use of the family group conference as a mechanism for producing a negotiated community response, and the involvement of victims as key participants, making possible a healing process for victim, offender and the community."[7]

The process is workable in cases where the accused admit guilt and the victim is willing to participate in the deliberations about a just settlement. To be truly successful, it also depends upon the presence of mature representatives of the larger community, facilitators

---

7. Jim Consedine, *Restorative Justice: Healing the Effects of Crime* (Lyttelton, NZ: Plowshares Publications, 1995), p. 99.

who can assist all of the participants in an unfamiliar and quite difficult process, and government officials who see their role as enablers
of a process of healing rather than as dispensers of punishment. In his
book *Restorative Justice,* Jim Consedine describes the system at work in
the example of a sixteen-year-old boy apprehended for stealing six
cars in one day:

> He met with representatives of his family, the police, the De-
> partment of Social Welfare and four of the car owners in a fam-
> ily group conference. . . . After opening with karakia (a prayer),
> the kaumatua (elder) of the family spoke of his embarrassment
> that one of his nephews had got himself into so much trouble.
>
> [The constable] read out the summary of facts. This in-
> cluded the information that one of the cars had a front fender
> damaged and another had interior damage. The young man
> then admitted the offences, saying that he had been "out of it"
> on drugs at the time. One car owner angrily said that didn't help
> him get to an important meeting on time and he had ended up
> paying $56 for a taxi. Another said he had appreciated the
> youth's guilty pleas but wondered whether the whole episode
> might not be repeated once this case was over. A third said that
> he had lost his $200 no-claim bonus from the insurance com-
> pany and wondered how the youth felt about that.
>
> The coordinator said that it was up to the group to arrive at
> a suitable penalty. After further discussion among family mem-
> bers, who spoke of their experience of the youth, his inability to
> make friends, and his waywardness at school, the family retired
> to discuss what they thought an appropriate penalty might be.
> After a cup of tea the conference reconvened and the family put
> forward their proposal. They suggested that the youth repay
> both the money for the no-claim bonus and the taxi fee. Further
> to that, he agreed to see a counselor with a view to entering the
> Odyssey House drug programme.
>
> He accepted the offer of one of the car owners to be taught
> to drive properly and eventually got a license. In exchange, he

agreed to cut that owner's lawns each Saturday during the following summer. All present agreed on this procedure.[8]

While this case doesn't deal with violent crime, it has the compo-
nents of the vast majority of crimes committed in New Zealand, and
in the United States for that matter. The offender is a youth (less
than twenty-five), involved with drugs or alcohol, and the crime concerns property. In New York, approximately 75% of all crimes are related to drugs or alcohol, involve young people, and relatively small
amounts of property are at issue.

In New Zealand the process for young offenders differs mark-
edly from the system for dealing with adults who commit crimes.
There the British adversarial system holds sway, as it does in this
country. The victim is a silent bystander except when called as a witness. The battle is fought between two opposing lawyers, with the
state seen as the one primarily harmed, while the community or family has little or no voice except representatively and abstractly. The
emphasis in the adult system is upon punishment of the offender,
whereas the emphasis in the Children or Young Offender's Court is
upon the healing of the victim, the offender, and the community.

Native American Sentencing Circles

There are some strong similarities between the New Zealand approach to young offenders and the very old custom of Native American sentencing circles. The basic principle of the sentencing circle is
the same: everyone affected by the crime is to be involved — victim,
offender, the families and colleagues of each, and the larger community — for the sake of the healing of all participants. Sentencing circles also depend upon the admission of guilt by the offender, the
willingness of the victim(s) to participate, the presence of family and
supporters of each, representatives of the larger community, and

8. Consedine, *Restorative Justice,* pp. 98-99.

some court professionals. The role of the professionals is to facilitate the discussion and decisions rather than to control them, as is true in our standard court system. The participants agree to meet until the process is complete and a consensus is reached.

In the sentencing circle victims and witnesses confront the perpetrators, who must deal with the shame that comes with the admission of having broken the community's mores. It is probably fair to say that the role of shame is much more significant here than in our traditional approach, which speaks of guilt more than shame. The perpetrators are also sensitized (many for the first time) to the impact of their actions on the victims as they hear from the victims, face to face, what happened to them and how it has affected their life. Frequently this leads to deeper remorse than that generated simply by having been caught and accused.

When all the parties who wish have spoken, then the victim, family and supporters, sometimes accompanied by helping professionals, meet separately to discuss what they consider to be an appropriate sentence. Often sanctions are demanded, such as community service or even occasionally some form of imprisonment. Some form of reparations or restitution is also usually required, depending upon the nature of the crime and the circumstances of the perpetrator. The sentencing circle makes recommendations about ways to help heal the perpetrator, including such things as counseling, alcohol or drug abuse assistance, and training in nonviolent patterns. In some cases underlying social factors are involved, such as unemployment or lack of educational opportunities, which may be addressed to the larger community with specific recommendations to correct the problem. The sentence is brought back to the full circle where others, as well as the perpetrator, are invited to respond. The final sentence must be a consensus.

Some form of sentencing circle is common to many traditional tribes throughout the world, and the practice has met with a variety of governmental responses. The Canadian criminal justice system has recently recognized sentencing circles as appropriate in many criminal situations — generally in all but the most violent cases. The state still reserves the right to override the sentence imposed by the circle, but such usurping of the community's power is infrequent. In the United States, Native American communities have had greater control over their justice systems because of the greater degree of overall self-government recently granted them, so various forms of the sentencing or court circles are quite common. Their jurisdiction, however, is largely limited to civil matters rather than felonies.

Those outside Native American communities widely assume that the practice of sentencing circles is primitive, quaint, ineffective, time-consuming, and impractical in criminal matters. While it is true that, in many cases, all the participants may be involved for three or four days before a consensus is reached, this pales in comparison to the extraordinary length of some of our more notorious trials. And, in order to avoid our lengthy trials, many cases never go to trial, left to plea-bargaining instead. In New York City, almost 95% of all cases are plea-bargained. Even more fundamentally, those who favor the sentencing circles argue that the time is well worth the result: the healing of the community. There is no shortcut to healing.

It can seem unfair to some that perpetrators should have a say in the matter. Nevertheless, such an attitude fails to recognize the humanity of the perpetrator and the necessity for the healing of everyone, not just the victim. Just as in the physical healing process, those who are not well need to participate as fully as possible in the process to maximize the healing.

Another challenge comes in allowing the victim, the perpetrator, and those connected with them to set the sentence, because emotions may override wisdom in such a setting. In the Canadian system there is a safeguard, albeit seldom used, against this possibility. Court professionals have the right to overrule the sentencing circle's judgment if they feel that the potential future danger to the community has not been sufficiently considered.

Restorative Alternatives Inside
the Dominant U.S. System

Within the United States, as in New Zealand, the juvenile courts have led the way in developing approaches to justice that go beyond simply punishing the perpetrator. Recognizing that many youthful offenders have received inadequate or inappropriate socialization, education, and supervision, the state has sought to find ways to hold families and public caretakers accountable. Mark Moore describes the role of the juvenile court not as a criminal court dealing with crimes committed by youth but rather as a civil court "responsible for administering a body of law that regulates the conduct of parent and other care givers as well as children."[9] The juvenile courts have, in many cases, taken it upon themselves to oversee "the conditions under which children are being raised."[10]

The state of Oregon has recently passed a law that holds parents accountable for the misdemeanors of their children, a notion that has a long history going back to colonial times. This approach recognizes that the offender is part of a larger family system that must be considered and involved if rehabilitation and healing are to occur. One community in Oregon has developed a juvenile repayment program, in which the businesses of the community provide opportunities for the juvenile offenders to earn income in order to repay their victims.

Another alternative that recognizes the circle of complicity and accountability is the family group conference. Throughout the nation there is a host of new efforts to provide family and community input into the response to youth crime. California, Hawaii, Illinois, Iowa, Kansas, Michigan, Oregon, Pennsylvania, Vermont, and Washington are all, in a variety of forms, implementing family group conferences.

The essence of the family group conference is that the immediate

9. Mark H. Moore, "The Future of the Juvenile Court: A Theoretical Framework That Fits," *The Future of Children* 6, No. 3 (Winter 1996): 140.
10. Moore, "Future of the Juvenile Court," p. 142.

and extended family, as well as any identified support persons, are involved in discussion with the offender and the victim in assessing the harm done and the appropriate sanctions and reparation. Such an approach incorporates the dynamic of shame and broadens the responsibility for healing to the larger family and community, not simply to the perpetrator. The intent is to help families take responsibility for their children.

Another form of restorative justice that is increasingly used is Victim Offender Reconciliation (VOR). This occurs both inside and outside the prison walls and is facilitated by professionals, corrections' employees, and volunteers. The basic aim of VOR is to bring about reconciliation between victims and offenders. Steps toward that end include the sensitization of the perpetrators to the impact of the crime upon the victim, informing the victim regarding the circumstances of the perpetrator's background, a full disclosure of events that have sometimes become hazy in the mind of the victim, the opportunity for the victim to forgive the perpetrator, and the opportunity for the perpetrator to experience that forgiveness. Sometimes victims are unable to confront perpetrators face to face, so surrogate victims are used. Finally, victims and offenders often get assistance in negotiating a restitution agreement. The results can be dramatic; both victims and perpetrators speak of the power of talking openly and the moving experience of forgiveness. This is what the TRC in South Africa is discovering.

Some programs focus primarily on the rehabilitation of the offenders. While this is less than the full circle of healing that restorative justice calls for, it is nonetheless a step away from punishment and toward healing. According to a report of the National Center on Addiction and Substance Abuse at Columbia University, 80% of all those imprisoned in the prisons and jails of the United States are there for crimes related to alcohol and illicit drugs. Despite the fact that the provision of treatment is so clearly important, New York and many other states have severely cut back on such treatment in recent years. The study found that 840,000 federal and state prisoners needed drug treatment in 1996, but fewer than 150,000 received any care before being released. Joseph Califano, Jr., the chairman of the center, said that such inaction was "tantamount to visiting criminals on society."[11] When attention has been given to helping to cure addiction, the results have been dramatic. According to the New York State Criminal Justice Alliance, "quality drug treatment programs have consistently reduced recidivism 36-60%. . . . A RAND study found that drug treatment reduces serious crime 15 times more than mandatory minimums and 10 times more than conventional sentences. Another RAND study concludes, moreover, that six dollars in public funds were saved for each dollar spent on drug rehabilitation."[12]

There is also often a direct correlation between poor education and crime. Seventy-five percent of New York prisoners have no high school diploma, and forty percent cannot read. For many years the state offered GED (high school equivalency) and college education for those who qualified. After 1994, with the ending of the Pell grants that provided federal support for higher education, many states also cut back on expenditures for education. In some cases, such as New York, all support for higher education in the prisons was ended. These cutbacks and eliminations of programs and funding came despite the fact that it has been proven that the higher the education prisoners receive, the lower their recidivism rate. One study showed that in Texas, the recidivism rate for those without college degrees is sixty percent, while for degree holders the rate was only twelve percent.[13] Among the graduates of New York Theological Seminary's master's degree program, the recidivism rate is less than five percent. That program, while permitted and even encouraged by the state, has never received any state funds, and is fully supported by gifts. Some colleges, recognizing the enormous difference an education can make, have adopted this model and raised outside money to offer

11. Steven Belenko, "Behind Bars: Substance Abuse in America's Prison Population," posted Jan. 8, 1998, at www.CASAColumbia.org.

12. "Restoring Balance to Justice: Setting Citizen Priorities for the Corrections System" (undated publication, New York State Criminal Justice Alliance), p. 6.

13. "Restoring Balance to Justice," p. 9.

some coursework free to prisoners. To date, however, such efforts have been piecemeal. At this writing, there are two New York City area religious colleges that are preparing to expand their offerings significantly so that prisoners can obtain bachelor's degrees.

Restorative Justice in Minnesota

The state of Minnesota has moved in some significant ways to incorporate restorative justice throughout its criminal justice system. In November 1993, its Department of Corrections (DOC) became the first department in the nation to appoint a full-time employee to address the process of restorative justice. For many years, Minnesota has been a progressive state with respect to criminal justice, imprisoning a significantly smaller percentage of persons than most other states. In addition, its choice of police personnel and justice officials evidences a concern for a more humane approach to the problem of crime. Almost twenty years ago, Minneapolis selected Anthony Buza as the police chief. Tony Buza had been a district commander in the South Bronx, where he developed a reputation for fairness, an equal toughness on crime and police brutality, a concern that young police officers be trained to care for the community, and a willingness to tell the truth, no matter what the consequences. His criticisms of the punitive nature of police work and his challenges to work more closely with the community earned him the ire of some of his peers. With such a progressive leader in such a prominent position of law enforcement, it is no surprise that Minnesota responded favorably and institutionally to the idea of restorative justice.

The DOC set out to educate, model and facilitate a variety of initiatives that foster restorative justice practices. The response has been significant. According to a report by Kay Pranis, change has occurred both inside and outside the corrections system.

Most community-based corrections practitioners in Minnesota have been introduced to the restorative justice framework and many of them are exploring ways to implement the concepts. . . . Several innovative new community-based programs have been designed. . . . Knowledge of restorative justice has been incorporated as an expectation in the hiring and promotion process for some positions in the DOC. The DOC Academy . . . includes a session on restorative justice.

The DOC district supervisor of field services in Bemidji, Minnesota and the regional supervisor of Sentencing to Service . . . requested assistance in the development of a new community-based program built on restorative justice principles.[14]

She continues the impressive litany of actions with notations of efforts by the clergy, conferences for state legislators, training for judges, and community forums. As a whole, Minnesota is a leader in the movement toward restorative justice.

Problems and Limitations in Restorative Justice Programs

While there are many significant forays into restorative justice within the United States, there is yet no place in which restorative justice is the overarching framework for dealing with criminal acts, and herein lies a basic problem. Since restorative justice programs operate within an overall framework that is basically punitive, these programs are, at best, small reprieves from the grinding dehumanization of the punishment orientation. At worst, they serve as palliatives, allowing the basic punitive orientation to continue while giving a certain satisfaction in making small alterations.

There are debates about whether it is feasible to eliminate punishment. Some believe that there is no room for any punitive responses,

---

14. Kay Pranis, "A State Initiative Toward Restorative Justice," in *Restorative Justice: International Perspectives,* ed. Burt Galaway and Joe Hudson (Monsey, NY: Criminal Justice Press, 1996), pp. 500ff.

including capital punishment, solitary confinement, or even imprisonment. Lee Griffith has argued for the abolition of prisons from a biblical and theological perspective. He believes that prisons are counter to the Judeo-Christian heritage. "Cages, chains, pits, dungeons, jails and prisons are biblically identified with the power and spirit of death. They are totally and irrevocably renounced."[15] Michel Foucault asserts that prisons are ultimately part of the destructive power dynamics of an oppressive society. Prisons are essentially about punishment. Foucault claims that there can be no restorative role for prisons as they essentially serve to "normalize" those imprisoned, which means that they are coerced into a pattern of behavior that fits the basic power arrangements of the society.[16] Others have argued that imprisonment and other sanctions are sometimes needed to protect the community. Still others believe that there is room for some punishment when it is set in the context of an essentially restorative approach.

What is the "Re" in Restorative?

Many prisoners in my seminary's Sing Sing program have raised questions about the "re" in restorative and rehabilitative. How can we be rehabilitated, they ask, when we have never been habilitated? The basic issue for them is habilitation. To habilitate means to enable, having to do with the notion of enabling capacity or qualification. As most of our prisoners in the United States are poor and persons of color, it goes without saying that societal enabling has not been their common experience. When they do achieve, they do so against great odds.

It is impossible to argue that the experience of people of color in

---

15. Lee Griffith, *The Fall of the Prison: Biblical Perspectives on Prison Abolition* (Grand Rapids: Eerdmans, 1993), p. 188.

16. Michel Foucault, *Discipline and Punish: The Birth of the Prison,* trans. Alan Sheridan (New York: Vintage Books, 1979), esp. pp. 128-131, which conclude a historic examination of alternative purposes served by punishment and the contemporary emergence of coerced conformity as the goal rather than restoration. The following section on "Discipline" analyzes imprisonment as a mechanism of conformity.

our society is one that has been habilitating and a condition desirable to restore. In the 1940's, a number of black children were given black and white dolls to play with in order to determine their preferences. A majority of the black children chose white dolls, because they considered them better or more beautiful. It is clear from that experiment that these children had not been habilitated into healthy self-affirmation.[17] The even greater tragedy is that when the exercise was repeated thirty years after the achievements of the civil rights movement, the results were almost identical. When children literally are forced to run the gauntlet between warring gangs simply in order to get home from school, they have not been habilitated into a healthy, trusting approach to life. When economic resources and meaningful job opportunities have been removed from the community, the residents have not been habilitated as persons of hope.

Dr. Welile Mazamisa, in a criticism of the TRC process in South Africa, commented that the whole notion of restoration "means going back — what is required in South Africa is to go forward."[18] Within his critique was a recognition of the reality that the "re" in restoration and rehabilitation assumes that there is a former situation worthy of recovery. In the case of South Africa and for most of those imprisoned in the United States, the former condition most certainly is not what we wish to recover. We have to begin with habilitation.

What is at stake is the transformation of the society as well as the criminal justice system. In that regard, it may be more accurate to speak of transformative justice rather than restorative justice. The advantage of this terminology is that it points to the fullest circle of redemption necessary to deal with the reality of crime — the entire arena of social justice, including economic and political justice. The disadvantage in referring to the task as transformative justice is that it may lead us into a

17. K. B. Clark and M. P. Clark, "Racial Identification and Preference in Negro Children," in *Readings in Social Psychology*, ed. T. M. Newcomb and E. L. Hartley (New York: Holt, 1947), pp. 169-178.

18. "South African Council of Churches Conference on Reconciliation and Healing: The TRC and the Church" (report on conference held in Johannesburg, Oct. 23-25, 1996), p. 33.

rather amorphous project that takes the focus off of the current retributive justice system and its egregious consequences. Whatever terminology we use, it is important to realize that what is involved is the necessity of a fundamental change both in our society's response to crime and in our society's failures that help to cause crime.

It is clear that the "re" in restore and rehabilitate is more related to an ideal that has not yet become a reality than to the actual circumstances of many lives. That is where the Genesis creation narrative fits in. The power of the creation account in Scripture is precisely that it claims a condition against which to judge all other conditions. It is an ideal, set in mythic-poetic form. Its truth lies precisely in its power to capture our imaginations and to draw us to the utopian vision. It is an originating myth that has the power to point toward the telos, the end goal for which we all strive. It is not a lost condition to which we are to be restored, but a metaphor for a condition intended by God and for which we long.

Despite the differences among those who call for the abolition of prison and those who seek to make it rehabilitative or restorative, there is agreement that anything short of a restorative approach to criminal justice is inadequate and doomed to failure. The basic limitation of restorative justice as it is now practiced, however, is that often the circle of redemption is incomplete. We must deal with the issue of habilitation. Just as some would argue that it is impossible to have truly restorative justice by introducing some restorative programs into an essentially punitive framework, so I would argue that even a fundamentally restorative approach to crime cannot succeed without attention to the broader societal issues of habilitation. Only as society understands that one of its fundamental roles is to be the guarantor and provider (at least of last resort) of the resources necessary to live a full life will it be possible to speak authentically of restoration. That is the bitter lesson of South Africa today. That is the bitter lesson of so many prisoners who have been released only to find less than whole lives on the outside.

The failure to recognize this truth has contributed to the international spread of the spirit of punishment. One paper reviewing international activities in the field of sentencing and corrections claims that "the fundamental problems facing the criminal justice systems of the world are so similar that there is much agreement as to the outcome of adhering to the present discredited policies and practices." Among them is "a fearful denial of society's responsibility for crime prevention, education and social justice [that] leads to the expectation that the criminal justice system alone will provide a solution."[19] The United Nations Declaration of Human Rights, the United States Constitution, the Bill of Rights, and various other forms of legislation all serve to move us in the direction of human rights. Nevertheless, rights exist in the context of basic economic systems, and in a market economy the rights of capital too often override the rights of persons. In fact, it can be argued that the United States Constitution, while in some ways a model of human rights in the world, is nonetheless more geared to property rights than to human rights. Even with the best of legislation, the power to interpret the law naturally rests in the hands of those already empowered in other ways.

This is the danger that South Africa faces today. An essentially restorative approach to crime is in place; the rights of all are being assiduously sought and protected. But political guarantees and incentives regarding human rights are not enough. In the absence of genuine economic democracy, the means to provide adequate resources to habilitate the majority of the people are lacking. As a result, antisocial and thus anti-reconciliatory criminal behaviors are increasing, predictably leading to a call for greater punitive measures.

Authentic restorative justice demands a truly habilitative society, and that entails a transformation of the broadest kind. Each alternative that I have discussed is important and can contribute to a more healthy society. Yet each in itself or even all of them together cannot bring about full restoration. For that to happen, we must find ways to address the larger social constructs within which criminal justice plays its part.

19. Neville H. Avison and Yvon Dandurand, untitled background discussion paper for the May 1995 Ninth World Congress of the International Centre for Criminal Law Reform and Criminal Justice Policy, Vancouver, B.C., Canada, p. 2.

| | |

CHAPTER FIVE

Amazing Grace:
Foundations for Restorative Justice

Restorative justice, or the circle of redemption, looks principally to the future rather than to the past. It seeks more to rebuild than to cut out — that is, it is not primarily surgical, but curative. Our current approach to criminal justice, not unlike much of our current medical system's approach to sickness, focuses upon removal of the unwanted elements. It is surgical — cut and burn. In some ways it is similar to bloodletting, which was based on the belief that by removing the offending elements healing would occur. Unfortunately, the patient often died and the anxious family became the grieving family.

Our nation seems fixated on the notion that if we can remove the offending persons from society, we will have taken care of the sickness. A retired police officer and former schoolteacher recently suggested to me that we send all those convicted of serious crimes into an outer space colony and let them fend for themselves. There are several fundamental problems with this "lock them up and throw away the key" mentality. The first is that because crime is of such epidemic proportions, we will find ourselves removing more and more people to "clean up" the society. While the economic costs of this approach are staggering, the costs to family life and community life are even more pronounced. A wide circle of family, friends, co-workers, and neighbors is intimately affected for every person who is removed from society. Two million prisoners translates into 15 or 20 million people whose lives are torn asunder. The costs borne by the children of those who are removed are passed down through the years, like the ancillary effects of surgery upon surrounding tissue, muscles, and nerves.

Clearly there is a time for surgery — for removal — but we have used the surgical approach almost exclusively. Our asylums and sanatoriums for the mentally and physically ill have been largely surgical. We have removed the offending elements from the "healthy" society for as long as they needed to be removed — sometimes forever — often with little attention either to the restoration of the "offending one" or to the trauma for those intimately connected. Our response to those who commit crimes is similar.

In a striking contrast, many traditional cultures understand healing to involve restoration rather than removal: for example, the Qechua of South America, many African nations and tribes, and the aboriginal peoples of Canada, the United States, and New Zealand that were discussed in the previous chapter. Each offers not only an alternative way of dealing with offenders that has been loosely captured under the term "restorative justice," but also a radically different foundation for creating social policy. This fundamental difference in understanding the world is of ultimate importance.

Restorative models of justice are built upon philosophies or worldviews that understand all of life as sacred, interconnected, and interdependent. They see all of creation as a circle. Separating any aspect of life from all other aspects, any form of life from all other forms, any living thing from all other living things, is impossible. There is a universal umbilical cord, which cannot be severed. This makes it difficult, if not impossible, to think of cutting out and discarding anyone in surgical fashion.

The notion of life as a circle, in which everything is connected, is in stark contrast with the dominant Western worldview shaped by the Enlightenment. Our approach to reality is far more dichotomous. We understand things as in *or* out, this *or* that, rather than as in *and* out, this *and* that. We socialize our children into this dualistic mode of thought and behavior that is antithetical to their natural way of being in the world. When we observe very young children, we see that for them the lines are not so clearly or permanently drawn. Boys and girls play together with little or no sense of gender lines. They have to be taught that racial differences matter. They mix together the emotive and the rational seamlessly as they solve problems and fantasize. One day's foe becomes the next day's friend. And so it goes.

One way in which I have become aware of the inextricable connection of life is through the painful process of divorce. While ending a marriage is possible legally, divorcing oneself relationally is impossible. We carry our relationships with us, whether through the connections that continue in the sharing of children or the internalized responses to life that have been shaped by the original relationship. There is a similarity in kind, even if not necessarily in extent, to our internalized responses to our parents, our classmates, and our friends. Each of us has had the experience of responding to current circumstances as if we were responding to a relationship in the past, as if it were our parent or friend being affected or watching us, even though we thought that we had left them behind long ago. This is even true when we are separated by death. It is impossible to share deeply and intimately without being indelibly and forever affected.

While *ontos* (being) is essentially one for traditional societies, much of Western thought and practice views being in a dualistic manner, assigning essential distinctions and a hierarchy to those distinctions. It is not enough that there is a difference between men and women, blacks and whites, and so on, but these differences are considered essential; therefore, one must be better than the other. Because we consider some things as ontologically different (i.e., fundamentally different by nature, in their very being) there is a temptation to categorize some as superior and others as inferior.

This idea of ontological superiority and inferiority is not the same as the acknowledgment of differences. Differences are inevitable and they may lead to an assignment of value, but this need not imply ontological status. Some differences are functional. Clearly a shovel is better for removing dirt from the ground than is a coat rack, but no one would assume that the shovel is therefore ontologically superior. It is simply better for accomplishing a certain purpose.

Other differences are aesthetic and can be enriching. Upon arising, I find Mozart better suited for my mood. In the evening I might prefer Fauré. This does not make one ontologically "better" than the other, though I might say that I like one better than the other. Too often we confuse the line between aesthetic tastes and ontological claims. Cornel West's genealogy of racism points to the danger of such confusion as he traces one of the roots of racism, the combination of modern scientific observational skills with Greek notions of beauty. This combination led to a valuation based on phrenology and provided justification for the assignment of inferiority to people of color.[1]

Aesthetically, it is undeniable that we are attracted to certain people on the basis of physical characteristics and personality traits, though it is interesting to note how our tastes are the product of a socialization that serves certain interests. To see size, shape, color, voice tone, or carriage as denoting superiority is as destructive as Hitler's ideology of the pure Aryan race. Our aesthetic preference does not make one person superior to another. The problem is that when we make the assumption that differences are ontological and then go on to assign value to the differences, it becomes easier to consider removing that which we consider inferior.

Assigning ontological status to differences is a crucial foundation of the historic racism of our society, and one of its most virulent contemporary forms is our criminal justice system. More than 80% of all prisoners in New York are people of color — most of them poor. Perhaps that is why it is so easy for many middle- and upper-class whites to talk about locking "them" up and throwing away the key. It would not be so easy to discount and discard the other if our own children were under consideration. It would not be so easy if the perpetrator were an educated, middle-aged white woman whom we had known as a neighbor rather than an impoverished young man of color who

1. See Cornel West, *Prophesy Deliverance* (Philadelphia: Westminster Press, 1982), Chapter 4.

has been hidden behind Berlin-like walls that ghettoize "us" from "them."

Many cultures and traditions affirm the essential unity of all beings. Among those traditions is the Judeo-Christian faith, or at least some branches within that faith tradition. Many traditions outside Judaism and Christianity affirm the same kind of unity as well, rejecting the notion of essential differences in being. Though each of us has specific roles to play, no person is fundamentally less valuable than any other. We turn now to some of these traditions, first outside the Judeo-Christian faith and then within it.

Ubuntu

Having been trained in an Enlightenment-oriented education, I found it particularly challenging to step outside the box and learn something of a traditional African philosophy/spirituality known as *Ubuntu*. The Ubuntu philosophy has been instrumental in shaping South Africa's response to apartheid, one of the most remarkable restorative responses to crime in our contemporary world. South Africa is particularly important because its restorative approach to crime is set in a contemporary nation-state that is modern in many significant ways. Unlike the many aboriginal tribal cultures that have survived at the margins of dominant nations, South Africa is itself a dominant nation.

Ubuntu, a fundamental form of African spirituality, is a word rich in meaning and almost impossible to translate into a direct English equivalent. It does not translate easily into English, and many do not attempt to translate it at all. It is an elastic word because of its richness. "Ubuntu Botho" has been roughly translated as "African Humanism."[2] It goes well beyond simply a concern for the human community to an understanding of the connectedness of all life forces. One Ubuntu community in South Africa speaks of Ubuntu growing out of

2. See "History and Philosophy of the Inkatha Freedom Party," http://www.ifp.org.za.

"the organic relationship between people, their spiritual roots, and the natural world, and resting on the following insights:

- Humanity is an integral part of ecosystems, leading to communal responsibility to sustain life.
- Human worth is based on social, cultural, and spiritual criteria and competence rather than conventional market-based conceptions.
- Natural resources are shared on principle of equity among and between the generations."[3]

This broad-based understanding of the interconnectedness of all of life is reflected in the Ubuntu saying "Umuntu ngumuntu ngabanye abantu," which is translated "a person is a person by and because of other people."[4] Such a philosophy emphasizes the goodness, dignity and integrity of all persons and affirms our mutual dependency.

Desmond Tutu, a member of the Xhosa people, openly acknowledges his indebtedness to the philosophy of Ubuntu as one of the shaping factors in his own theological and spiritual orientation:

> In the African Weltanschauung, a person is not basically an independent solitary entity. A person is human precisely in being enveloped in the community of other human beings, in being caught up in the bundle of life. To be is to participate. The summum bonum here is not independence but sharing, interdependence. And what is true of the human person is surely true of human aggregations. . . .[5]

As one author points out, for Tutu this interconnectedness is the *imago Dei,* evident from the very beginning as God creates man and

3. International South Group Network, South Africa, formerly at www.mbnet .mb.ca/linkage/consume/ubuntu.html (January 1998).

4. www.ifp.org.za.

5. Michael Battle, *Reconciliation: The Ubuntu Theology of Desmond Tutu* (Cleveland: Pilgrim Press, 1997), p. 39.

woman for relationship with each other, God, and all the inhabited earth. This interconnectedness has implications for the political order, emphasizing care and responsibility for all inhabitants of a given society.

It is almost unfathomable how people who have been brutalized, treated as animals, denied elementary rights, and sometimes had members of their family tortured and killed could possibly forgive the perpetrators of those crimes. Yet in South Africa, time after time, people who have suffered such atrocities have embraced their enemy and offered forgiveness. Underneath such grace often lies the philosophy of Ubuntu.

Ubuntu's impact is evident in Africa's widely diverse Christian and secular religious communities. Its adherents include members of various African tribes, President Mandela, many members of the ANC, and Bishop Desmond Tutu, the chair of the Truth and Reconciliation Commission. Ubuntu's sense of unity offers a striking challenge to the Enlightenment heritage of Cartesian dualism. Ubuntu is a chief cornerstone of the Truth and Reconciliation Commission's mission to bring healing to that bitterly divided nation.

I do not mean to discount the detractors and critics of the TRC, some of whom allege that many of those who offer forgiveness have been manipulated, pressured, or cajoled. Until my early twenties, I was heavily involved in fundamentalist Christianity, and my own experiences with mass evangelism indelibly impressed upon me how people can be led into actions they would never undertake on their own. It is quite conceivable that the charismatic presence of Bishop Desmond Tutu, the public nature of the hearings, and the general hope that forgiveness will be forthcoming could combine to have a similar impact upon some of the victims of apartheid.

Nevertheless, in many cases the forgiveness is real, however unfathomable that may be to us. I spoke with mothers whose children had been killed, to a priest who had lost both hands to a letter bomb, to a man who had been systematically harassed and tortured by the Afrikaner police, and to others who had suffered similar treatment. Yet somehow they found it possible to forgive. Their forgiveness was neither gullible nor cheap. Some still felt deep bitterness, and many were critical of the limitations of the movement toward justice. Nevertheless, most felt that there would be no peaceful and healthy future for their grandchildren if the circle of violence were not broken, if former enemies could not find a way to treat each other as humans. They understood that they were inextricably linked with each other — even with their victimizers — and that life could not be made whole without forgiveness. In part, their understanding was rooted in the philosophy of Ubuntu.

Native American Spirituality

Native Americans also have a spirituality and philosophy that provide guidance in all matters of life, including their response to crime. The ethicist and social historian Robert Craig has done extensive research into the native communities of North America, with special reference to their idea of law, justice, and community. Instead of the adversarial approach characteristic of Western jurisprudence, the underlying assumption among Native Americans is that the people are essentially one — including perpetrators, victims, and community. Craig points out that the meaning of law is best defined as "the way to live together most nicely." He goes on to say that "what captures the essence of the Mohawk legal system is 'peacemaking'; a healing process that involves communication, listening, and the wisdom to seek solutions that are non-adversarial." For the Lakota and Dakota people, "what sustains the lives of people are bonds of kinship relations that bind human and nonhuman together with a sense of mutual responsibility and caring." He quotes the Lakota phrase *Mitakuye Oysain* ("all are relatives").[6]

Chief Seattle's letter of 1854 to United States President Frank-

---

6. *Thunder in My Soul: A Mohawk Woman Speaks* (Halifax: Fernwood Publishing, 1995), p. 225, as quoted in Robert H. Craig, "Institutionalized Relationality: A Native American Perspective on Law, Justice, and Community," *Annual of the Society of Christian Ethics* 19 (1999): 294-95.

lin Pierce makes clear this sense of inextricable connectedness. In response to the United States government's offer to buy land from the tribe and to resettle them to a reservation, the chief was incredulous about the notion of selling the land. While some controversy surrounds the exact wording of the original letter, he clearly expressed the Native American belief in the connectedness of all of life and wondered at the notion that humans — only one part of the web of life — could buy and sell other parts of that web.[7] That sense of the connectedness of all of life typifies the dominant Native American spirituality, and has led to remarkably humane approaches to criminal justice, as we have seen. When people understand their essential connectedness, their ontological connection, forgiveness is possible.

Judeo-Christian Roots

While there are many potential sources for an understanding of essential human interconnectedness, dignity, and worth, one does not need to adopt an African philosophy or Native American spirituality to arrive at such conclusions. There are many images and metaphors within the Judeo-Christian tradition that point toward the same conclusion. Three that are especially foundational for restorative justice are belief in covenant, the Incarnation, and the Trinity. I would be the first to admit that these are not the most self-evident choices when setting forth a foundation for restorative justice. Certainly they are not as accessible to the average person as are the notions of forgiveness and reconciliation, each of which makes major contributions in the same direction.

7. There are many versions of this letter. The first newspaper account of the letter was published in 1887 and is available in the Washington State Archives. The specifics differ in each version, but all assume the same underlying philosophy of oneness with the land and the impossibility of escaping from our interconnectedness. The United Methodist Worship Book uses part of this text for its liturgy on environmental justice.

Currently, forgiveness is receiving a good deal of attention, and with good reason. Recently a number of very important and helpful books have appeared dealing with forgiveness and reconciliation from theological and ethical perspectives. Donald Shriver, in the legacy of Niebuhrian realism, offers a compelling treatment of the need for a politics of forgiveness.[8] Willard Swartley's edited volume, *The Love of Enemy and Nonretaliation in the New Testament,*[9] offers us a rich exploration of New Testament texts that deal with stories and teachings related to forgiveness, non-violence, and love of enemy. Gregory Baum and Harold Wells have compiled a volume that explores the churches' responses to ethnic conflicts around the world, showing how forgiveness is made manifest in circumstances of extreme animosity and alienation.[10] Miroslav Volf has provided us with one of the most comprehensive treatments of the theology of forgiveness, or what he calls the "embrace of the other." His work arises out of the crucible of the ethnic conflict in Croatia and his faith. For him, the key is in what he calls the self-donation of God in Jesus Christ. His task is to seek "to explicate what divine self-donation may mean for the construction of identity and for the relationship with the other under the condition of enmity."[11]

In spite of all these important contributions, there are several reasons why I do not think that focusing upon forgiveness is sufficient. The first is related to the distinction raised by the prisoners between habilitation and rehabilitation. If they are correct, and I think they are, then this raises a question as to who needs forgiveness. Certainly the one who has committed a criminal act is in need of forgiveness from the victim and the larger society that has been harmed. But so

8. Donald W. Shriver, Jr., *An Ethic for Enemies: Forgiveness in Politics* (New York: Oxford University Press, 1995).

9. Willard Swartley, *The Love of Enemy and Nonretaliation in the New Testament* (Louisville: John Knox/Westminster Press, 1992).

10. Gregory Baum and Harold Wells, *The Reconciliation of the Peoples: Challenge to the Churches* (Maryknoll, NY: Orbis Books, 1997).

11. Miroslav Volf, *Exclusion and Embrace: A Theological Exploration of Identity, Otherness and Reconciliation* (Nashville: Abingdon Press, 1996), p. 25.

too is the society in need of forgiveness for having created and permitted crime-generative communities to exist. If the lack of habilitation is a reality, then those responsible for this condition are as much in need of forgiveness as is the perpetrator of any specific crime. Often criminal acts are destructive responses by individuals to the sins committed against them. The child who is battered, sexually abused, provided with second-rate education and no employment opportunities not surprisingly may turn to battering and abuse as an adult.

Andrew Sung Park distinguishes between *han* (a Korean word for the pain of the wounded heart that is destroyed by evil acts) and sin (the acts that harm victims and cause *han*). He rejects the dominant Christian notion that treats the pain of the victim *(han),* with its attendant responses, as equivalent to the act of the oppressor (sin): "Sin is the volitional act of sinners (oppressors); han is the pain of the victim of sin."[12] With this understanding, Park suggests that forgiveness by the oppressed must always be linked with repentance by the oppressor. If we accept that premise, we should not move to the notion of forgiving the perpetrator of a criminal act without at the same time recognizing our need for repentance for creating the conditions that foster criminal acts. Both are in need of forgiveness, and both are in need of repentance.

The second reason why focusing on forgiveness is inadequate is that there is an underlying problematic that must first be addressed. Almost everyone believes in forgiveness. We know the social and personal benefits that occur when we forgive others and help them toward a new path. They are affirmed and given a fresh start, and we are freed of the bitterness that accompanies harbored resentments. Together we are free to rebuild and deepen our relationship. The reality, however, is that there are only certain people whom we find it possible to forgive. While we believe in forgiveness, we are often limited in our understanding of who deserves it. That is why, despite the increasing discussion of forgiveness, reconciliation, and nonviolence

12. Andrew Sung Park, *The Wounded Heart of God: The Asian Concept of Han and the Christian Doctrine of Sin* (Nashville: Abingdon, 1993), p. 12.

in published literature, retribution still rules the day. Although most of us have heard the injunction of Jesus to forgive seventy times seven, we seem incapable of forgiving under certain circumstances; even when we know we should, we find it almost impossible. Many of those calling angrily for the death penalty are devout members of churches who are familiar with the injunction to forgive but understand it to pertain to a different circumstance. The call for forgiveness has often fallen on deaf ears.

It seems to me that our difficulty in forgiving is linked to our fundamental assumptions about life, and especially about certain people. We can find it in our hearts to forgive some people time after time, often for even egregious actions, but there are others we find it impossible to forgive. Frequently this difference in response is related not so much to the nature of the offense as to the nature of the offender. When the offender is one of us, it is quite different from when the offender is "other," or one of "them."

Only when we discover our interconnection will we be able to move beyond the distancing, brutalizing, punitive spirit that characterizes much of our society. Within the Judeo-Christian tradition are resources for such a transformation, and if we are able to understand them in fresh ways, they may provide a foundation for our openness to forgiveness and reconciliation. Each of the three underscore our inescapable need for each other — including the least "desirable" among us.

Covenant

The notion of covenant goes back to the very early origins of Israel and perhaps even beyond to the city-state kings who entered into agreements with peasants and herdsmen for protection in exchange for payment and services. Israel understood its origins as a nation to come from God's covenant with Abraham, through whom God intended to bless all the peoples of the earth. God promised to free the people of Israel and give them their own land in exchange for faithful worship and living. The Christian church, building upon this ancient covenant, came to believe that in Jesus Christ a new covenant had been instituted, one that built upon and fulfilled those that preceded it.

Covenant was one of the most important teachings within the fundamentalist tradition in which I was raised. Our local church was part of the dispensationalist movement, a theological tradition that began in mid-nineteenth-century England. Using a literal interpretation of Scripture combined with numerology and a strong apocalyptic sense, dispensationalism developed a biblical theology that divided all of history into a series of covenants between God and humans. Each covenant, such as the Adamic, Noahic, or Abrahamic, represented a different epoch in human history, defined by different goals, different ways in which God was revealed, and different demands, with each superseding the previous one. We believed that the culminating age or dispensation will be the millennium — God's direct rule on earth. We engaged in heated debates about when the battle of Armageddon would occur and whether the second coming of Jesus would occur before, during, or after the millennium. We carefully delineated every age or dispensation with literal proofs from both testaments of the Bible, especially the apocalyptic writings of Daniel and Revelation. We believed that God revealed the pattern of history with exactness, and that any faithful reading of Scripture would uncover it, so that the faithful could know the pattern. By our calculations, the last days were now upon us. All the signs pointed to the end of history.

As time went on, I came to understand the Scriptures, God, and human history in much less simplistic ways. But behind that arithmetical, sequential, and rigid way of viewing history as a series of covenants lies, I think, a profound truth: God and humans live in an ever-changing relationship. We experience our relationship to God in many different ways, but always as covenant. The trouble with dispensationalism wasn't its recognition of the multiplicity of covenantal relationships, but rather in its assumption that one form supersedes another for all time and that there is a formal, rigid pattern to the history of these changing covenantal relationships.

The ancient image of covenant is a particularly powerful challenge for a culture that has become overwhelmingly individualistic. For our society, the notion of the commonweal or common good has largely given way to looking out for our individual needs and desires. We see this abnegation of responsibility for the common good at every hand. Corporations walk away from commitments to their workers and the communities in which they have long resided, leaving despair and depression in their wake. Marriages end as if the continuity of children were not an issue, with countless fathers refusing to honor their commitments to their children. Taxpayers and representatives who are concerned only about their own bottom line vote to cut any social program if doing so seems expedient.

A covenant can be simply an agreement or contract, such as a transfer of title to a piece of property. However, in the biblical sense, it also involves a commitment to an honoring of the other party. In the narrative relating the origination of Yahweh's covenant with Israel we are told that Abraham was chosen and blessed in order to be a blessing. Scripture recognizes that the covenant is more than simply an agreement or vow — it is the instigation of a saving dynamic. Whatever legalities may be involved are in the service of a blessing upon others or even upon the whole cosmos. The biblical notion of covenant is always salvific, always for the sake of the shalom of the person, of the nation, of the world, of the cosmos, of God.

With this concern for well-being and a healthy relationship characterized by shalom, it is inevitable that covenants change, because such relationships are based on mutuality and reciprocity. While some, such as Calvin and Barth, have emphasized the importance of the origination of a covenant with God, I find the emphasis upon reciprocity much more crucial. It is not so important who originates a covenant as how it is worked out and continually reworked by both parties. In our deepest loving relationships we enter into covenants — marriage is one of them. It could be either partner who takes the first step, who woos and pursues. Nevertheless, it is only as the two respond to each other that a true relationship builds. Each response becomes the occasion for the response of the other, each response a new initiative.

In the Calvinist tradition, there has been such emphasis placed upon God's initiation of the covenant that the understanding of reciprocity has often been lost. Seeking to affirm the sovereignty of God, Calvin emphasized that God initiates everything, even our ability to respond openly. With such an emphasis, the reciprocal movement from human initiative to God as responder got lost. Yet the writers of Scripture over and over again portray the covenant as moving back and forth between God and humans. Even when God is portrayed as the initiator, which is more often the case, Scripture tells of reciprocity. Some of the earliest covenant narratives demonstrate this. Cain, the murderer of his brother Abel, was granted safety after pleading with God that his punishment was greater than he could bear. In response, God placed a mark upon him, guaranteeing that he would not be killed (Gen. 4:15). Abraham bargained with Yahweh over the destruction of Sodom and Gomorrah (Gen. 18:23-33). The story of Jacob wrestling with the angel (Gen. 32:22-32) is one of the most marvelous examples of the reciprocity of covenant, where Jacob refused to obey God's command to let go, and demanded that God bless him in exchange for letting go. God's response to Jacob's bold request was to change his name to Israel, "for you have striven with God and with men, and have prevailed" (Gen. 32:28). Jacob, in the custom of the times, named the place where this event occurred Peniel, saying, "For I have seen God face to face and yet my life is preserved" (Gen. 32:30).

How dare Jacob act in such a manner? What right did he have to challenge God? Jacob was a liar, a schemer, and a thief. He had stolen his brother Esau's birthright by exploiting his brother's weakness, by lying to his dying father, and by using the religious ritual of the final blessing to usurp what rightfully belonged to his brother. For years he lived as a fugitive, exiled from his brother's land, cut off from his family. When he recognized the tragedy of his condition, he resolved to make things right with his brother, and began the first step toward restoration of the relationship. It was then that he met the stranger who wrestled with him all night. In honoring the covenant with his brother, Jacob was free to experience the fullness of his covenant with God. Even a criminal has the right to claim his or her dignity and worth before God and others in the context of reciprocity. The dynamic of the covenant is that we are in relationship with God and with each other, and we have the right to make claims, assert our needs, and present our desires, just as others have toward us.

The demand of covenant is mutual accountability. Those of us who are concerned for restorative justice must be careful not to lose sight of this fact. It is too easy to fall into the mentality of noblesse oblige, thinking that we are here simply to help prisoners. The reality of covenant is that we are implicated with each other, we are shaped by each other, and each response in this relationship changes us all. We cannot escape the fact that when one is harmed, all are harmed; when one is imprisoned, all are somehow trapped. Similarly, when one is healed, all experience healing; when one is built up, all are stronger; when one is rehabilitated, the society becomes more habitable. The inescapable fact is that we *are* our brothers' and sisters' keepers — and they are ours. We bear accountability for our actions to our brothers and sisters, no matter who they are or what they have done. Just as God was willing to be held accountable to Jacob, we are called to be accountable to the entire web of life. Many of us have come to understand that we are also accountable to the environment — air, water, natural resources, and all species. If we are able to understand that nature holds us accountable in a covenant of reciprocity, perhaps we can discover the capacity to be held accountable by those sisters and brothers who have committed crimes.

Our criminal justice system operates primarily on a premise of one-way accountability. The perpetrator is tried, convicted, and sentenced based on his or her failed accountability to the larger society. Yet the society has largely failed to understand its accountability to the person who becomes a perpetrator. The almost predictable link between poverty and criminal behavior should lead us to question the accountability of both the private and public sectors in addressing issues of economic development, job training, quality public education, decent affordable housing, and many others. When we as a society begin to acknowledge the reciprocal accountabilities that link all of us, we will be a step closer to shalom, which is the goal of covenant.

Incarnation

Christians claim to experience the revelation of truth incarnationally in the person of Jesus Christ. This metaphor and its implications are what makes us distinctive from all other religions, but the distinction need not involve an exclusive or unique claim about God's revelation in Jesus, although it does for some. It is sufficient to understand that while some find truth in other places, Jesus is definitive for us.[13]

Incarnation, from the Latin *incarnatus,* means "made flesh." To speak of God's Incarnation in Jesus is to claim that we discover God in the flesh, in a human — in this case in Jesus of Nazareth. There is nothing uncommon about the man Jesus. He is from humble circumstances, of a birth questioned as illegitimate, from a small town. When we trace his lineage, it consists of both royalty and prostitutes — nothing special. He was just a common man, but in him "the fullness of God was pleased to dwell" (Col. 1:19).

Doctrinal debates about Jesus and the nature of God's Incarnation in him have continued since the days of the early church, including debates about the virgin birth, the presence of sin in Jesus, his relationship to both God the Father and the Holy Spirit, the significance of his death, the nature and meaning of the resurrection, his return, and his current status. Most of the early debates were couched in language that is difficult to understand today. The defining moment was reached at Chalcedon in 451, four centuries after Je-

13. For a fuller exploration of this issue, see John Hick and Paul Knitter, eds., *The Myth of Christian Uniqueness: Toward a Pluralistic Theology of Religions* (Maryknoll, NY: Orbis, 1995), and Scott Cowdell, *Is Jesus Unique? A Study of Recent Christology* (New York: Paulist Press, 1996).

sus' death and the birth of the early church. The Council at Chalcedon said the following:

> Therefore, following the holy Fathers, we all with one accord teach men to acknowledge one and the same Son, our Lord Jesus Christ, at once complete in Godhead and complete in manhood, truly God and truly man, consisting also of a reasonable soul and body; of one substance with the Father as regards his Godhead, and at the same time of one substance with us as regards his manhood; like us in all respects, apart from sin; as regards his Godhead, begotten of the Father before the ages, but yet as regards his manhood begotten for us men and for our salvation of Mary the Virgin, the God-bearer; one and the same Christ, Son, Lord, Only-begotten, recognized in two natures without confusion, without change, without division, without separation. . . .[14]

The idea of God appearing to humans in incarnate form is quite old. In the Jacob story, the one who wrestled with Jacob was called a man, but when the blessing was given to Jacob, the stranger revealed that Jacob had been wrestling not only with a man but also with God. Elsewhere we have the story of God appearing to Abraham by the oaks of Mamre (Gen. 18:1-22), this time in the form of three strangers. These strangers ate and drank with Abraham and predicted that 99-year-old Sarah would give birth the following spring. Overhearing this, Sarah laughed "to herself" and expressed incredulity. The strangers asked Abraham why Sarah laughed and questioned their promise. They responded, "Is anything too hard for the Lord? At the appointed time I will return to you in the spring and Sarah shall have a son." Note the use of "I" by the three strangers, their ability to hear a silent laugh, and their understanding that it is the visitation from the stranger that will empower the birth, a use of power

---

14. Henry Bettenson, ed., *Documents of the Christian Church,* 2d ed. (London: Oxford University Press, 1963), p. 73.

that is generally understood in the Bible to be within the province of God alone. In Luke 24:13-35 we have a similar occurrence, this time with the risen Jesus. Two disciples were walking on the road to Emmaus, despondent because of the crucifixion of their master. A stranger joined them, someone they did not recognize, and they began to talk. Not until they shared a meal together did it become clear to them who this stranger was — the risen Jesus. And then, like the man who wrestled with Jacob and the strangers who visited with Abraham, he vanished.

In the Bible, God is spoken of as being encountered in natural phenomena such as a bush, the roll of thunder, the beauty of the natural environment, the majesty of the eagle, the donkey (Balaam's ass), a common meal, and dreams and visions. The Incarnation asserts another point of encounter with God: in human form, in flesh, in a particular person. The question is whether God's self-disclosure is limited only to Jesus or if God is incarnate in other or even all persons.

I recall hearing of a pastor who was driving through Brooklyn and stopped at a red light. As he was waiting for the light to change, a man came up to his side window for a handout. It was a bitter winter day; the man had no coat and was quite chilled. The pastor ignored the man and kept his eyes fixed straight ahead to avoid making eye contact. The man left and went to the car behind, a taxicab. The pastor watched through his rearview mirror as the driver got out of his taxi, took off his coat and put it on the man. "That morning I met Christ twice," the pastor said, "once in the man begging and once in the driver who shared his coat." Martin Luther spoke of our responsibility and opportunity to be Christ to our neighbor. I believe he was right. The corollary is also true — our neighbor can be Christ to us. There is no one to whom we cannot be God's presence, and there is no one who cannot be God's presence to us.

It is impossible to grasp the full truth of the Incarnation. The reality of the Incarnation is that we meet God in the common stuff of life. For many Christians the most expected, most likely place to encounter God is in the rituals and rites of the church. As with Roman Catholicism, which developed a hierarchy of callings, the most sacred of which is the calling to the priesthood, followed by religious orders, and finally the laity, Protestantism has its own operative hierarchy for how we meet God — and it is generally in the realm of the religious rather than the everyday that the encounter occurs. The Incarnation destroys this hierarchy.

There is a danger in thinking of ourselves as the bearers of Christ. When we seek to minister out of our abundance and privilege we sometimes lose sight of the possibility that God will visit us through the stranger, the outcast, the vilified, even the criminal. We may think we are "Christ bearers" to them, but often it is the other way around. God continually surprises us by being incarnate in the least-expected persons.

The Incarnation demands that we respect the "other" as the one through whom we can meet God face to face. It also invites us to anticipate God's revelation in the unexpected. Because of God's Incarnation, we are obligated to be open to finding truth, beauty, and worth from the most unanticipated quarters. We are obligated to respect the stranger who is the image of God in flesh for us.

I can attest to the presence of God in women and men in prison. Not just the brilliant ones, not just the "nice" ones, but through many different ones who have revealed the truth about life to me, who have revealed love and beauty and dignity in the face of the most dehumanizing odds. Like Sarah, I have at times responded with incredulity, doubting that anything life-giving could happen. I have questioned whether anything good could come out of Sing Sing. Nevertheless, God has spoken through the least expected, the least of these, my brothers and sisters.

Trinity

The doctrine of the Trinity is the most complex and perplexing doctrine within Christianity. It defies all logic, is extrapolated rather than drawn directly from the Scriptures, was a late development in formal Christian theology, and has engendered more controversy than any other doctrine. As with all doctrines, its importance in the life of the church has at times risen to prominence while at other times fallen into obscurity.

The temptation facing the church has always been to collapse God into a monism or to affirm multiple gods. An early proponent of the Trinity was Dionysius, Bishop of Rome (around 260 A.D.). His critical letter to Dionysius of Alexandria tries to hold the tension between these two extremes.

> In this connexion I may naturally proceed to attack those who divide and cut up and destroy that most revered doctrine of the Church of God, the Monarchy, reducing it to three powers and separated substances and three deities. For I learn that there are some of you, among the catechists and the teachers of the Divine Word, who inculcate this opinion, who are, one might say, diametrically opposed to the view of Sabellius; he blasphemously says that the Son is the Father and the Father the Son, while they in a manner preach three Gods, dividing the sacred Monad into three substances foreign to each other and utterly separate. For the Divine Word must of necessity be united to the God of the universe, and the Holy Spirit must have his habitation and abode in God; thus is it absolutely necessary that the Divine Triad be summed up and gathered into a unity.[15]

This letter is a precursor of the orthodox formula adopted at the Council of Nicea in 325, the first ecumenical Christian council. Constantine deemed the enormous divisions that were present within the church to be a threat to the peace of the Roman Empire. His interest in reaching an agreement had little if anything to do with theology, but was motivated by personal and imperial concerns. In fact, at the time he presided over the Council of Nicea, he was not yet a member of the church.

Again, it is not my purpose to articulate a complete doctrine of

15. Bettenson, *Documents of the Christian Church,* p. 45.

the Trinity, but to explore the possible implications of the notion of Trinity as a basis for restorative justice. My own understanding of the metaphor of the Trinity is related to the historic problem some have described as the problem of the one and the many. The two most logical solutions to the problem have led to either monism, in which God is all and all is God, or dualism, in which there is a radical ontological separation between God and all else. The doctrine of the Trinity seeks to hold this tension together in a paradoxical manner. It is not necessarily logical; it is born out of experience.

People have claimed to experience God in such a variety of ways that a pantheon of deities is quite understandable. Israel's monotheism was born as a challenge to the notion of multiple gods. Within early Judaism this tension was not completely subsumed. The plural name for God, *Elohim,* continued to be used, and one of the titles for God was Lord of Hosts. Indeed, throughout the history of Judaism and Christianity there has always been a tension between God as one and God as many.

In the early church, the problem was compounded because they thought that the singular creator God was present also in Jesus of Nazareth, the savior, and in the form of the Holy Spirit, who indwells all believers. To give full deity to each of these three and yet not revert to multiple gods required some creative philosophical and linguistic gyrations.

For me, the importance of the notion of the Trinity is not to be found in its theoretical explanation but in its imagery depicting the fundamental nature of the basis of reality (which is God). In the doctrine of the Trinity we have a recognition that reality, in its most essential form, is relational and loving. One consequence of this way of talking about God is that we understand God as always existing in community. God is fundamentally relational.

Such a notion goes hand in hand with Martin Buber's paraphrase of John 1:1, "In the beginning is relation."[16] To understand God as

16. Martin Buber, *I and Thou,* 2d ed., trans. Ronald Gregor Smith (New York: Scribner, 1958), p. 18.

Trinity is to claim that all reality is essentially relational, inescapably relational, forever relational. The trinitarian idea parallels the interconnectedness of Ubuntu or the spirituality behind the sentencing circles of the native peoples.

The doctrine of the Trinity speaks of a reality that demands the disposition of receptivity. No person, indeed nothing in the universe, is outside the circle of the essential connectedness of being. We are all ontologically related to one another, no matter what our distinctions. As Gabriel Marcel put it, we are invited into "disposability."[17] To be disposable to others is to incline ourselves toward them, to make ourselves ready to receive them. Disposability is the essential requisite for both loving and praying.

There are several images of this disposability in Scripture that support the trinitarian development. Jesus speaks constantly of "doing my Father's will." In the Garden of Gethsemane, when he is sweating blood in fear of his impending death, he prays that the Father will let this cup pass from him. Nevertheless, when all is said and done, he is willing to do the Father's will. In a similar vein, the role of the Holy Spirit in prayer is spoken of by Paul as being that of one who takes our unspeakable longings and groans and carries them to the Father. These sighs "that are too deep for words" (Rom. 8:26) are understood by the Father, who responds to them faithfully. Only persons who are in deep relationship are able to communicate at such a level. Close friends, lovers, and parents and children can often communicate with unspoken gestures and seemingly meaningless words or even sounds. The ability for such "sighs" to communicate, rather than simply to be taken for nonsense, grows out of profound intimacy and disposability.

The demand of a trinitarian understanding of God is that we be in such

---

17. Gabriel Marcel, *Creative Fidelity*, trans. Robert Rosthed (New York: Farrar, Strauss and Company, 1964), esp. pp. 38-57. According to Rosthed, "There does not seem to be any single word in English which adequately renders the French *disponibilité*. The term is generally translatable as availability — spiritual availability in this context, i.e. openness to the other, readiness to respond, forthrightness, etc." (translator's note, p. 57).

intimate relation with others that we are disposable to their sighs. This is difficult to imagine with respect to those who commit crimes. Most of us have been socialized into thinking that our connectedness ends with our similarities or our comfort zone. Anyone outside the comfort zone or who is deemed "different" is easily considered disconnected, of a different order or quality. Categorizing people as "other" allows us to treat them in a manner that is alienated and alienating. If the distinctions within the Trinity were those of "other," there would not be one God but three, and alienated ones at that.

The Trinity provides us with an image of God as three distinct persons who are so intimate and loving that they are one. We are invited to be in the same relationship with all that is. All beings are part of us. Just as to speak of Trinity is to speak of God loving within God, so we are invited to understand that to love another is to love yourself, and to hate another is to hate yourself. And because everything is connected, to love another is to love God, and to hate another is to hate God. We are inextricably united — even in the differences that constitute our most personal characteristics. That we are essentially one with each other, even those whom we fear or whose actions we despise, is no more difficult to grasp than the notion of the Trinity.

To understand our lives as essentially and intimately connected with all other living beings, including God, poses a serious problem for those who hold to a doctrine of the fall that implies total depravity and the loss of the image of God. For them the essential connection has been lost. For them, restoration can occur only when the individual's heart is regenerated through conversion. All other tasks are secondary to proclaiming this truth and inviting persons to make the decision to turn to God.

Such an understanding can lead to sympathy for those imprisoned, but it does not necessarily or even logically question the spirit of punishment. In fact, apart from the rebirth of the individual criminal, the assumption is that prisoners fully deserve punishment and, with the final judgment, all who have not accepted Jesus will be punished eternally. This understanding leads to a form of evangelism that fails to deal with the policies of our criminal justice system or the spirit of punishment that dominates our culture. Rebirth, like rehabilitation, is assumed to be for the individual prisoner alone.

It is impossible to remain within such a narrow and reductionist understanding of the task of evangelism when we understand the nature of both creation grace and redemption grace. The circle of redemption leads us to a broader understanding of evangelism, of the good news of Jesus Christ.

| | |

CHAPTER SIX

Getting Well:
Completing the Circle of Redemption

A Fuller Understanding of Evangelism

With few exceptions, such as the Mennonite Central Committee and the Society of Friends, which have consistently been in the forefront of penal reform, the churches of our nation have largely abrogated their responsibility for dealing with criminal justice. While many denominations have offices dealing with criminal justice issues, they are generally small, understaffed, underfunded, and marginal to the overall life of the denomination. Generally, staff and budget are extremely limited and local church interest is spotty. The voices of the dedicated few who keep the issue alive largely have been drowned out by those with other concerns. On the policy front, most denominations have contented themselves with occasional pronouncements about capital punishment, giving priority to rehabilitation and similar ideas. Yet serious public education, lobbying, and organizing efforts have been rare and have received limited support.

The last major push by my own denomination was in 1988, following a General Assembly pronouncement that was quite prophetic.[1] The moderator, Ken Hall, sent the pronouncement and an

1. Rev. Kathy Lancaster, Director of the Presbyterian Criminal Justice Program,

enclosed letter inviting response to governors, legislators, and criminal justice professionals throughout the United States. The response was encouraging. Many of the leaders in the criminal justice arena wrote back agreeing with the tenor of the pronouncement and asked for support in their struggle to move toward restorative justice. Little has been done since. A decade later, our prisons are fuller, more prisons are being built, more persons wait on death row, and the spirit of punishment continues to spread like a virus.

The silence of most churches and individual Christians is born out of a failure to understand the full meaning of evangelism, the sharing of the good news. The task of engaging and addressing our criminal justice system is one of the major evangelistic challenges facing the churches of the United States today. To speak of this task as evangelization may appear strange to some. Is this not social justice ministry? Don't we mean outreach and mission rather than evangelism? Evangelism in the context of criminal justice primarily has meant a focus on the individual souls of the incarcerated. While the conversion of persons who have committed crimes is a critical component of the evangelistic thrust, it is far too limited an understanding of all that is implied by evangelism.

At the center of Jesus' ministry was the proclamation of the Good News, the evangel. He was an evangelist above all else. In him we witness a life dedicated both to pointing to and being the way, speaking and doing the truth, revealing and living the essence of life ("I am the way, the truth and the life," John 14:6). The fullness of the Good News he brought was revealed in his first recorded public comments, offered in the Temple. In the custom of the elders of his day, he read a portion of Scripture selected for the day and then commented upon it. The text he read from Isaiah is particularly appropriate for our interest in crime, criminals, and the nation's response:

---

and those who have worked with her are exceptions to the general apathy in the Presbyterian Church USA regarding criminal justice. Her ongoing work, commitment to restorative justice, and perseverance in the face of an overwhelmingly disinterested church stand as a beacon of hope.

The Spirit of the Lord is upon me, because he has anointed me to preach good news to the poor, he has sent me to proclaim release to the captives and recovering of sight to the blind, to set at liberty those who are oppressed, to proclaim the acceptable year of the Lord. . . . Today this scripture has been fulfilled in your hearing. (Luke 4:18-21)

This text has been interpreted by many to support a traditional style of personal evangelism in which visitors go into the prison to tell the imprisoned about Jesus. During my high school and college days I participated in this kind of evangelism. We were completely focused on winning prisoners' souls, oblivious to the totality of conversion needed: a conversion of the prisoner, the prison, and the broader society. We understood the problem as one of personal sin with no recognition of the systemic evil involved. Our understanding of salvation was a narrow one — preparing prisoners for heaven after death. Such a limited proclamation of the Good News is more like an excerpt than the full story.

This notion of evangelism fails to understand the wider circle of redemption to which Jesus pointed when he quoted Isaiah. He spoke of both proclaiming and setting free, in keeping with the core biblical tradition of redemption encompassing the totality of life. Time after time, redemption is described in Scripture in holistic terms that involve words and acts, persons and structures, spirits and systems, heaven and earth.

Jeremiah 33 offers us a wonderful image of the meaning of righteousness, the completing of God's intention for the world. The prophet received a vision of what would happen to his nation, then in ruins:

In this place, of which you say, "It is not fit for man or beast, in the cities of Judah and the streets of Jerusalem that are desolate . . . there shall be heard again the voice of mirth and the voice of gladness, the voice of the bridegroom and the voice of the bride, the voices of those who sing, as they bring thank offerings to the house of the Lord. . . . For I will restore the fortunes of the land as at the first," says the Lord. . . . "There shall again be habitations of shepherds resting their flocks . . . flocks shall once again pass under the hands of the one who counts them." . . . And the name by which it will be called: "The Lord is our righteousness."

Jeremiah's vision offers us several clues for understanding the scope and consequences of the evangelistic task. The first clue is that the restoration involves the whole of life. Family life is restored, with marriages again flourishing. Public life is restored, with the streets ringing with mirth and gladness as they are given back to the people. Worship life is restored and the rituals take place again in the house of the Lord. Finally, economic life is restored, as the shepherds no longer work for the benefit of foreign owners but control the sheep themselves. The redemptive vision of Jeremiah involved the entirety of the society and its inhabitants: culture, politics, religion, and economics.

The Isaiah text with which Jesus identified himself is of the same magnitude. It is concerned with those who are poor and in captivity due to indebtedness or foreign occupation, with those who are sick and in need of healing, and with those who are oppressed in any form. The scope of Isaiah's vision requires proclamation and preaching, touching and healing, economic action and politics. Such an all-encompassing vision cannot be accomplished with a truncated approach that focuses only on individuals.

The text ends with the proclamation of the Year of the Lord, the Jubilee year that was to occur every fifty years, at the end of a Sabbath of Sabbaths. During the year of Jubilee, or Year of the Lord, all prisoners were to be released, all debts canceled, all land returned to its original owners. It was a totally new beginning, a wiping clean of the slate. Sharon Ringe has elaborated on the extensive presence of this theme both in the Hebrew Scriptures and in the ministry of Jesus.[2] She points out that the nature of the redemption was holistic, involving persons, structures, religion, eco-

---

2. Sharon H. Ringe, *Jesus, Liberation, and the Biblical Jubilee* (Philadelphia: Fortress Press, 1985).

nomics, families, and society. It was the creation of a new heaven and a new earth, the return to the way God had intended, as pictured in both the originating myths of creation and the culminating myths of the apocalypse.

It is inconceivable that we should understand the Good News at the beginning of the twenty-first century in any less holistic a way. The plight of so many of the poor, of people of color, of the youth — locked up in warehouses and treated like animals — parallels Jeremiah's description of the desolation that came upon Judah; it was "not fit for inhabitants or beasts." The gospel we have to proclaim must address the full scope of our reality if it is to be more than simplistic sound bites.

The second clue from Jeremiah's vision is that the restoration involves the very foundation of life itself, namely God. The name of the restored city is: "the Lord is our righteousness." Righteousness here is better translated as justice. As the *Harper's Dictionary of the Bible* points out, "The pervasiveness of the concept of justice in the Bible can be veiled from the English reader by the fact that the original terms most approximating justice have been frequently translated in English as 'righteousness' and 'judgment.' A rule of thumb can be that when these terms appear in a context of social distribution or social conflict, 'justice' would be a better translation."[3] Jeremiah recognizes that God's very being is wrapped up in the redemption of the people. God's identity, future, and integrity are all at stake. A restored world is God's longing as much as it is ours. God's righteousness and our righteousness are linked.

Care for the Victims

The Gospel of Matthew contains one of the most compelling images of final judgment and calls to justice in all of literature. Gathered be-

3. *Harper's Bible Dictionary,* ed. Paul J. Achtemeier (San Francisco: Harper, 1985), p. 557.

fore the throne are all the nations, called to account for their actions. Jesus commends some and condemns others. The commendation and condemnation are each related to the same reality — the treatment of the mistreated, the aid offered the ailing, the care given to the castoffs. "O blessed of my Father, inherit the kingdom prepared for you from the foundation of the world; for I was thirsty and you gave me drink, I was a stranger and you welcomed me, I was naked and you clothed me, I was sick and you visited me, I was in prison and you came to see me" (Matt. 25:31-46). Incredulous, those commended inquire when they acted so caringly to Jesus. His answer is momentous: "as you did it to one of the least of these my brothers [or sisters], you did it to me" (Matt. 25:40).

This portrayal of apocalyptic judgment offers several clues for the churches' response to crime. First, there is care for the victims. The church has often been at the forefront of binding the wounds of those who have been injured, giving shelter to the homeless, food to the hungry and open arms to the rejected. The stranger is welcomed and made to feel at home. These acts of hospitality are part of the historic pattern of Christian charitable and mission activities, often referred to as social service.

In recent years, social service has come under much criticism for its failure to address the deeper issues such as poverty, racism, sexism, and other forms of oppression. Concentrating on the more immediate and easier-to-address needs through soup kitchens, shelters, and clothing drives has led some to ignore the root causes of the injustice. It is possible for such acts to be merely Band-Aids that do no more than momentarily cover up the fundamental injury to persons and society. Churches in particular often have responded only to immediate individual needs, often having neither time nor resources nor inclination to deal with the underlying issues.

However accurate this criticism may be, we must not oversimplify matters by ignoring the immediate needs of people while we go about the business of radical change. It is impossible to be truly human and walk by the person who has been wounded and left by the side of the road, as Bertolt Brecht understood:

I hear that in New York
At the Corner of 26th and Broadway
A Man stands every evening during the winter months
And gets beds for the homeless there
By appealing to passersby.

It won't change the world
It won't improve relations among men
It will not shorten the age of exploitation
But a few men have a bed for the night
For a night the wind is kept from them
The snow meant for them falls on the roadway.

Don't put down the book on reading this, man.

A few people have a bed for the night
For a night the wind is kept from them
The snow meant for them falls on the roadway
But it won't change the world
It won't improve relations among men
It will not shorten the age of exploitation.[4]

While attention to the roots of injustice cannot be ignored, neither can our response to the victim in our midst.

Our model of criminal justice largely ignores the victims. The focus is on the perpetrator and the state whose laws have been violated. For the most part, the involvement of victims is only as witnesses for the prosecution. The pain they suffer is seldom directly addressed. Often victims are forced to relive the crime through the interminable processes of the criminal justice system, few resources are available for their own healing, and they remain silenced on the sidelines. Only rarely do they play any role in determining an appro-

4. Bertolt Brecht, "A Bed for the Night," in *Bertolt Brecht Poems — 1913-1956* (New York: Methuen, 1976), p. 181.

priate response to the crime. I have heard of many cases in which the victim or the victim's family has pleaded for leniency only to be ignored by the courts.

Many victims of crime find themselves as isolated as the prisoners. The bars behind which they live are invisible but just as strong as those holding the criminals, making escape difficult or impossible. Often feelings of shame accompany the trauma of victimization, especially for sexual crimes. Guilt, fear, and rage are common experiences for the victimized. Victims find it difficult and sometimes impossible, in their day-to-day relationships, to deal with their feelings openly and in ways that could contribute to release and healing. Some need professional therapy, which is beyond the ability of most congregations to provide.

However, there are many levels in the healing process, some of which churches can provide through the ministry of hospitality. It is not by accident that we call places of healing hospitals. True hospitality is needed for healing to occur. Churches can do many things to serve the process of healing. Without assuming the role of a professional therapist, selected church members can be trained by skilled therapists to be attentive listeners and to create safe spaces within which feelings can be expressed without being judged. In addition to trained individuals providing a listening ear and caring presence, churches can form victims' support groups. Churches have historically offered hospitality to Alcoholics Anonymous and other groups that serve a therapeutic function. Some churches have begun to do this with victims of crime.

Many of our churches are filled with victims of abuse or other crimes suffered at the hands of spouses, parents, partners, and acquaintances, but few find the courage or an environment conducive to sharing their ordeal. In a culture of silence they bear their burden alone, unaware that they are surrounded by others with similar experiences. Their hurt, shame, and rage smolder destructively inside them, waiting for an opportunity to erupt. We can begin to break this silence through our corporate prayer life, sermons, film discussions, and other possibilities. From those intimations may emerge broader conversations, programs, and victims' groups that begin to share and help one another.

The religious education programs for children in our churches offer an often overlooked opportunity for addressing this kind of need. Within our communities, there are many children who are the victims of violence or witnesses to it. Some of our churches are filled with children who have nowhere to turn to talk about the horrors and the fears with which they live. A sensitive religious education program can build the opportunity for these buried stories to surface and to set the stage for the next steps in the healing process. There must be a space, a home for people, including children and youth, who have been victimized to begin to deal with the fears, guilt, and rage that haunt them. A church can be such a home.

We are not totally unaware of this need within our society. There are times when the needs of victims are so clear that they cannot be ignored. When the tragic massacre of schoolchildren in Littleton, Colorado occurred, one of the first steps taken was to provide grief counseling for the children and their families. Everyone recognized the enormous impact of the trauma upon the students. It was not only those who were killed who were victimized; everyone involved was a victim. Many of the survivors and witnesses of violence suffer their trauma in silence. Healing requires a space and process for articulating their deepest feelings, and an invitation to share a safe space is good news to victims.

Hospitality for the Perpetrators

One of the most basic, easiest, and most rewarding acts anyone can do is to spend time with those who are imprisoned. It doesn't change the system or the plight of prisoners, but it can change their lives and the lives of those who visit them.

Prisons isolate. They are designed that way. The incarcerated are shut off from all normal human contact with family, friends, and the larger society. What contact there is is severely limited and circumscribed by time, space, and constraints of protocol. There is no natural flow. Everything must be carefully planned, approved, and controlled. In many cases, even the flow of information through letters and the media is restricted or censored.

Despite the comments one hears about some prisons being country clubs, there is nothing pleasant, humane, or welcoming about most of the prisons in the United States. Prison life is composed of small sterile cells open to public view, double and triple bunking in cells designed for one person, crowded dormitories, regimented schedules, sometimes brutal treatment, frequent sexual violations — including over twice as many rapes as of women nationwide[5] — limited opportunities for self-expression and self-improvement, body counts, strip searches, identification by number rather than name, impenetrable walls topped by razor wire, and guards with sticks and guns. It could hardly be more inhumane.

There is so much that visitors can do to counter the inhumanity and inhospitality of prison life. The warmth of a smile, the solicitation of a caring voice, the gentle touch of a hand on the arm, the hugs from a family member, prayer with a friend, a conversation unconstrained by fear — all these and more begin to restore the prisoner's contact with a broader, more healthy world and with a healthier self. I have also been struck by the importance of correspondence for prisoners. Many survive on letters, sometimes from persons they have never met except by mail.

Some churches have organized regular visitation programs and letter writing as part of their ministry. The Presbyterian Church of Rye, New York has been a partner in New York Theological Seminary's ministry at Sing Sing for many years. Each year, more members of that congregation have become part of a visitation program one or two evenings a month. They engage in Bible study, group dis-

5. According to Stephen Donaldson, President of Stop Prisoner Rape, their estimate of prisoners raped per year was 290,000, while the Bureau of Justice listed 135,000 rapes of women per year nationwide. *New York Times,* Dec. 19, 1993. While it is undoubtedly the case that the number of rapes reported by women far understates the reality, the enormity of the problem within prisons cannot be denied.

cussion, and private conversations. People follow up these visits with occasional phone calls and, more frequently, with letters. Friendships have developed, men have been warmly received and assisted upon release, and many of the visitors have become active lobbyists for prison reform.

A certain caution must be exercised when linking people on the outside with people on the inside, because some prisoners may take advantage of hospitable families. However, most of those who have been in our seminary programs at Sing Sing have proven to be trustworthy and not exploited those who visit them. Our program has become an informal and even unintended gatekeeper for learning the probability of successful contact. It is important that congregations and persons not enter into such relationships naively; where such a gatekeeping function does not exist, something similar to determine the probable appropriateness of contact is necessary. Prison chaplains can sometimes be helpful in this process.

The elderly are a largely untapped resource for the ministry of hospitality to those in prisons. Instead of lamenting that our churches are filled with the elderly, we need to see the rich potential they represent. This is particularly appropriate for ministry to those in prison. Many of us are so busy that we can communicate only by e-mailed half sentences or by cellular phones while driving or walking. The ministry of hospitality, whether in person or by letter, takes time — which many of our elderly have, along with prisoners. With extremely limited access to phones and other modern communications technologies, prisoners depend upon personal contact and letters. Our elderly can serve them well.

Our churches could organize the elderly to make visits and to correspond. Initially, the letter writing might be conducted through the church address, using only first names to preserve the privacy and security of church members. It is important that anyone volunteering to engage in this ministry of hospitality be trained to avoid the pitfalls of insulting superiority or naive vulnerability. It is vital that the relationship becomes neither *noblesse oblige* nor an opportunity to be tricked into foolish action. Still, these challenges should not dissuade us from the potential for providing a caring presence that offers welcome into our lives and enters, as much as possible, into the lives of the prisoners. We will find, in the process, that hospitality is a two-way street. The stranger often becomes the one who meets our needs as well.

When one has been denied a safe haven, hospitality is good news.

Hospitality for the Released

When men and women are released from prison, they return to a society that views them with fear, anger, and suspicion. The public fears that those who are released will return to the old ways that led them to prison in the first place. It is not an unfounded fear, as over half of those released commit crimes for which they are rearrested, convicted, and imprisoned. The recidivism rate in our nation is astoundingly high, leading some analysts to refer to prison as a revolving door through which the same people often pass two, three, or more times.

This is not surprising, for prison is not a place of restoration and rehabilitation, but a place of punishment. Rather than being prepared for a new way of life, most men and women in prison are simply biding their time until they get out. In New York State, the programs that could contribute to successful reentry in society are being systematically cut back: education, job training, substance abuse counseling, and other programs have in some cases been eliminated and in other cases reduced. Governor George Pataki's call for the end of parole to violent felons, if successful, would remove one of the incentives for rehabilitation and hope. With the emphasis upon punishment and a failure to seek rehabilitation, our prisons have become schools for training criminals. If those convicted of a relatively minor crime go to prison, the odds are that they will leave with few resources for successful reentry and a wealth of knowledge about how to commit major crimes.

Compounding the problem, upon release almost all return to the neighborhoods from which they came. That is what they are familiar with — family and friends are there, and they often have nowhere else to go. These neighborhoods, as mentioned before, are often crime-generative, characterized by low employment, crime, and inferior housing, schools, and public services. The odds are very much against someone being able to begin a new life in the presence of the influences that contributed to their criminal action in the first place, especially when they have been offered so little help in developing resources for success.

One of the major reasons those released from prison have nowhere else to go is that the larger society rejects them. Suspicion, fear, and rejection await them at every turn. With rare exception, once one is known as a former convict, it is an uphill battle to get a fair hearing, find a job, win trust, and be accepted as a normal human being. At every turn one faces closed doors — closed to jobs, to hearts, to homes.

Churches can become communities of welcome, whether they are in the old neighborhood to which the released prisoner has returned or in a new neighborhood. Some churches have adopted men and women while in prison and, upon release, taken them into their lives, helping them to receive job training, find housing, get a job, make friends, and build a new life. It is important that the adoption of a prisoner begin long before his or her release. The gap separating those on the inside from those on the outside is almost as insurmountable as the gap that separated the rich man and Lazarus. Stereotypes, misunderstandings, cultural differences, fears, prejudice, and ignorance all strain the tenuous relationship. Building a relationship that can survive for the long haul is an important task that takes time, patience, and understanding.

The return of most persons from prison to their own communities presents both a problem and an opportunity. Often the churches in these communities are themselves operating with extremely limited resources. On the other hand, there are churches in neighboring towns and counties with vast resources that could partner with one or more of the churches in the old neighborhoods to which most will return. This offers more affluent churches the very real, though less direct, opportunity to participate in the ministry of hospitality. Scarsdale and the South Bronx, Larchmont and the Lower East Side, Harrison and Harlem, can together open their arms.

One of the most effective efforts in the New York City area is the Exodus Project, housed and supported by the Church of the Living Hope in East Harlem in cooperation with several suburban congregations and numerous individuals. The project provides clothing, job interviewing and training, temporary housing, family orientation, and personal counseling to persons in transition. There are disappointments and pitfalls inherent in such a ministry. Those of us on the outside are often prone to be judgmental, naive, self-righteous, and controlling. Some of those who are released will fall back into crime despite the church's best efforts. Sometimes the largesse and welcome are received awkwardly and in a manner that is perceived as ungracious. Some persons may take undue advantage of the hospitality offered. But these risks go with the territory and don't differ from building any other relationship with the potential for blossoming or shriveling, becoming instrumentalist or reciprocal. The prodigal son's father had no way of knowing what his son would do upon his return, but he ran out to meet him with open arms, opened his home to him, and killed the fatted calf. We do not know the rest of the story. Did he take advantage of his father again? Did he revert to his former pattern? Or was he truly on the way to a new life? There are no guarantees; all we are given is the opportunity to welcome the prodigal home. While it is never ours to know the end of the story, the experience of many is that when hospitality and support are provided, new life flourishes. I can name a number of men who are living productive, loving lives because they have received the hospitality of a loving community.

Such welcome is good news.

A Cup of Water

The tragic state of our criminal justice system and our prisons is not simply due to some bad guards, uncaring wardens, tough police, and unsympathetic judges. The state of our criminal justice system is woven into the warp and woof of the larger society. Prisons are big business employing millions of people, run by governmental and, increasingly, private agencies. Prisoners perform labor at slave wages for government and corporate employers. Vendors, contractors, and many service businesses benefit from contracts with prisons. Communities in which there is high unemployment actively pursue prison construction as a means to provide jobs and stimulate the local economy. Federal and state laws set the guidelines for imprisonment and for the shape of the prisons themselves. It is impossible to deal with prisons and the criminal justice system without becoming involved with government and business. They go hand in hand.

Nevertheless, voluntary agencies and individuals can do some things to ameliorate the dreadful inhumanity and failures of the system as it now operates. While these will not change the system, they can provide some immediate relief to those imprisoned and to their families. Giving a cup of water to thirsty persons is only temporary relief if the well remains unavailable to them. Nevertheless, it may keep them alive until the day when the well becomes available. There are a number of measures that congregations and individuals can undertake to make life in prison more tolerable and potentially life-affirming.

One way to help is to minister to the more than one and a half million American children who have a parent in prison. Many of them are children of single mothers. Bedford Hills, a woman's prison in Westchester County, New York, has approximately 800 inmates. It is conservatively estimated that these women have two thousand children who are scattered in foster homes, living with relatives, and surviving on the streets. These children have very limited opportunity to be with their mothers, and in some cases never see them again. They are not allowed to live with their mothers in prison beyond one year of age. Each year, a number of individuals and several churches in the area of the prison serve as hosts to the children of the mothers in prison. For one or two weeks, the children stay in the homes of families in the area and each day they are taken to the prison where they can visit their mothers. It is only for a week or two, but it is a week or two they would never have except for this ministry.

We can also minister to the other members of the families of those incarcerated. Often prisons are so far removed from where the prisoner's family lives that it becomes prohibitive for family members to visit. Since seventy-five percent of all male prisoners in the state of New York come from seven neighborhoods in the city of New York, this means that most of those imprisoned are at least several hours from the city. Transportation is costly, time-consuming, and sometimes requires overnight stays for just an hour or two in the visitation room. Churches and individuals could arrange to transport visitors to and from the prison. Many churches have vans or buses that could be put to such use. Even in those cases in which there is public transportation from the city, some prisons are far removed from public transportation facilities, requiring expensive taxi rides from the station to the prison. Again, local churches and individuals could provide transport at little or no cost. The round trip from New York City to Auburn, Attica, and many other prisons cannot easily be done in one day on public transportation, necessitating an overnight stay. For persons on limited incomes, such expense is prohibitive. Hospitality in local homes can be provided for the families visiting the prison. Even for those who are incarcerated in prisons nearer to the city, hospitality for the families is a welcome event. Churches in the town of Ossining, where Sing Sing is located, offer refreshments, a quiet place to gather, and local transportation for the families who come to see their loved ones.

In the Judeo-Christian tradition, the ministry of hospitality plays a significant role. Some of the most dramatic instances of transformation in the Scriptures occurred when hospitality was extended. Even a simple cup of water is good news to a thirsty person.

Empowerment

In the face of a criminal justice system that does little to prepare men and women for return to society, many schools have offered educational and training programs inside the prisons. New York Theological Seminary offers the only master's program in religion in the United States to persons in prison — a forty-two-credit Master of Professional Studies in Religion degree. To be accepted, the candidates must have a bachelor's degree and show commitment to a faith community. Most of our candidates earned their B.A. or B.S. while in prison through one of the many programs offered by area colleges.

The experience at Sing Sing has been mutually rewarding for the prisoners and the New York Theological Seminary faculty. It has resulted in a deepening of our faculty's commitment to empowering the oppressed, to discovering truth at the margins, and to struggling for personal and social transformation. The graduates have learned new skills, sharpened their intellects, gained new perspectives, and deepened their faith commitments. As a result, they have found ways to use their training while in prison: as chaplain's assistants, as counselors, and as teachers in certificate programs. Our graduates are involved in such ministries in prisons throughout the state of New York. Upon release, many of them use their training in social service jobs, counseling, church-related work, or go on to seek ordination.

Following the federal government's elimination of Pell Grants, which supported post-secondary education in the prisons, New York and many other states also withdrew their funding for such education. Proponents of the cutbacks argued that prisoners were being rewarded with a free college education while hardworking, honest individuals had to pay to go to college. The argument struck a chord with many, contributing to the attitude that our prisons were becoming country clubs.

This decision was shortsighted by almost any measure. According to facts compiled by Citizens United for the Rehabilitation of Errants (CURE) in New York, offenders who engage in post-secondary education are far less likely to return to prison than those who don't engage in such a program. There is, by conservative estimates, at least a 20% reduction in recidivism among those who graduate from college while in prison. This results in a net savings of more than $30 million dollars per one thousand offenders completing the program — "an estimated potential net savings of at least $606 million per year nationally. . . . Every dollar spent on these programs yields at least four dollars in gross savings from lower operating costs and lower crime-costs alone."[6] Many prison superintendents in New York State openly speak of the foolishness of this decision, due to the potential unrest this may cause within the prisons. They strongly advocate the return of these or similar education programs.

In the wake of the termination of federal and state support for higher education in prisons, a few New York state colleges have been offering a limited number of courses for credit, without charge, raising outside funds and/or finding faculty to volunteer. New York Theological Seminary, which has never received state funds for its program, has raised the money every year. Bill Webber, director of the seminary's Sing Sing program, has been strongly encouraging church-related colleges to find ways to continue to provide this education despite the state's actions. Two colleges in the New York metropolitan area have indicated their intention of moving in this direction. Churches and individuals can financially support these volunteer efforts to provide education. For the untrained and uneducated, skills and education are good news.

Training in Alternatives to Violence

There is no more critical need in our society than a turning away from violence. Violence is at the heart of our society — the violence that produces the conditions for crime, the violence of the criminal act, and the violent responses to crime. Our prisons only reinforce the violence of the soul. It is absolutely essential that we understand the evangelistic task as a rebirth from violence into shalom, true peace. The abundant life that Jesus promised is a life with shalom at its core.

There is a nationwide movement to provide alternatives to vio-

6. Rudy J. Cypser, *The Pay-Back in Reducing Recidivism and Thereby Reducing Crime and Cost* (New York: CURE, 1997).

lence. Training is available both inside and outside the prisons, the latter to persons who have been released, at-risk youth, and families of the incarcerated. In these programs, men and women are taught how to deal with conflict and how to respond to violence around them without resorting to violence in response. Most of these approaches rely heavily upon volunteers with training and ongoing support. Many of the volunteers come from churches and synagogues that also provide facilities for the training and financial support for the program.

For those who know no response but violence, training in alternatives is good news.

The Public Face of Conversion

If our response to crime is to become truly restorative, it must go beyond loving care and volunteer programs. As important as these are, they are not the whole picture. Because the system is punitive rather than restorative, it needs to be changed fundamentally. The challenge to the nations in Matthew 25 inevitably raises the larger systemic issues.

First, it is important to end our reliance on imprisonment and to adopt the various successful alternatives that have been developed throughout the world, including within our own nation. This demands political conversion. Second, it is imperative that we address the causes of crime and not simply its manifestations. This demands economic conversion. Third, a spirit of healing and redemption must replace the spirit of punishment that drives our criminal justice system. This requires a conversion of the culture. Each of these changes represents a radicalism that can only be described as conversion — a fundamental turning around, an entirely new approach.

Public Policy and Culture

We dare not lose sight of the larger need by allowing the ministry to victims and prisoners to lull us into false satisfaction and to an abdication of our responsibility for the systemic issues — the problems of policy and problems of culture. Matthew 25, the Jubilee texts, Jeremiah 33, and other biblical passages offer us clues for this third dimension of response. They each point to the social-structural dimensions of redemption: setting free, eliminating oppression, ending poverty, and healing the disease.

In Matthew 25 we are told that it is the nations that are gathered in judgment. The term "nations" here refers to the collective community, and while it is not nation-states as we currently know them that are implied, the idea of the people as a whole is critical. Nations and communities can offer care and hospitality both through public works and through guiding principles and laws.

As we noted above, in the Jubilee text of Luke 4 and its predecessors, the Year of the Lord is concerned with economic rectification on a national scale. Each of the actions involved with Jubilee entails the use of laws and the power to implement them. In the restoration text of Jeremiah and others like it, it is the nation that is restored — involving governance, economics, and culture. The good news for persons inevitably extends to the good news for the nations. Public policy and the institutions of the collective community are as important to healing and redemption as are the personal decisions and actions of each individual.

The circle of redemption is holistic, so the task of the church in response to crime similarly must be all-encompassing. However, we dare not engage in the delusion that the church can act as if it were the center of the universe. The church has made that mistake in the past, creating the monsters of Christendom, holy empires, and state churches. An all-encompassing vision of restoration and redemption is not an excuse for imperialism. The church is but one of God's restorative instruments in the creation of a new heaven and a new earth. In Isaiah 40 we are told that Cyrus, the feared enemy King of Persia, had been anointed by Yahweh to set Israel free. The progenitors of salvation are many, varied, and often surprising. The church is but part of the struggle for justice and righteousness, part of the evangelistic task.

The enormity of the task drives us toward a new ecumenism, far broader than that of simply the Christian churches. We are called upon at once to claim our particular identity and also to recognize that God's grace is present and offered in many forms. To address the issues before us will demand the cooperation of faith communities that have too long been divided.

Public Policy and the Conversion of the Criminal Justice System

To speak of the conversion of the criminal justice system inevitably involves us in public policy. While it is impossible to legislate morality, it is certainly possible to create public policies that either enhance or impede justice, truth, and goodness. One cannot expect radical conversion through public policy developments alone, of course, since public policies are the product of debate and compromise. The best we can hope to do is to set a direction that, over time, might result in a fundamental paradigm shift from a punitive to a restorative goal. Our current policies are in need of fundamental conversion.

There are a number of critical policy issues that must be addressed. First, the law permitting capital punishment must be abolished. When we put someone to death, we have closed the door to redemption for both the perpetrator and all others who were involved: victims, family, friends, and community. It is common to hear families of victims say that the execution of a murderer brings their tragedy to closure. But that kind of closure is in itself tragic, for it eliminates the possibility for transformation, forgiveness, or reconciliation.

In addition, there have been too many innocent people who have been put to death or spent years waiting on death row. Jeffrey Blake was exonerated after spending one year in jail and seven years in prison for a double murder he did not commit. When the only eyewitness recanted, the case was reopened. His is only one of many similar stories. Governor Ryan of Illinois, a supporter of the death penalty, has recently called for a moratorium due to the excessive number of persons who have been convicted mistakenly.

And, even if guilty, if the perpetrator has become a transformed person before execution, what is to be gained by his or her death? Karla Faye Tucker, the first woman executed in the United States in decades, was evidently a changed person from when she admittedly killed two people in Houston in 1979. She was born again, and became a "model" prisoner. Despite pleas for clemency from people around the world, including the pope, Texas governor George W. Bush insisted on her death. Her circle of redemption cannot be completed now.

Arguments about the deterrent effect of capital punishment have proven empty. The majority of killings are crimes of passion. Knowledge of the death penalty cannot compete with the irrational emotions that drive crimes of passion. And for the rare cold-blooded professional killers, the death sentence is not a deterrent because they assume that they will not be apprehended, or that being caught is one of the risks of the business.

Our almost total reliance upon imprisonment for dealing with persons convicted of a crime covers over the fact that intermediate sanctions such as community service really are effective. Earned rehabilitation incentive programs help prisoners earn earlier release only if they meet rigorous standards of achievement. Shock incarceration is usually a three-stage program involving six months of intensive training and treatment for drug or alcohol addiction, an extended education and training period, and an outpatient aftercare period. These programs and others have proven to reduce recidivism, save money, and contribute significantly to the rehabilitation of perpetrators.

Parole is one of the alternatives that have worked well, media hype to the contrary notwithstanding. Parole allows a prisoner to live outside of prison while still under the supervision and care of the criminal justice system. Eligibility occurs when one has served the minimum sentence; it is theoretically based upon exemplary behavior, evidence of self-improvement while incarcerated, and the potential for a constructive societal contribution upon release. It provides strong incentive. For many sentenced for fifteen to twenty-five years, for example, the possibility of release after fifteen years has offered hope and incentive for good behavior.

But parole has become a political football. The media and many politicians have seized upon the occasional parolee who commits a notorious crime as evidence that parole is too grave a threat to the larger society. Seldom, if ever, do they mention that there are insufficient personnel to provide helpful guidance and supervision for parolees. Some individual parole offices have hundreds of parolees under their jurisdiction, making it impossible for them to provide the necessary assistance. New York's Governor Pataki, in a move in keeping with the mood of the nation, has vowed to end parole for persons convicted of violent felonies. Removing the possibility of parole obliterates hope. The continuation and creative expansion of the use of parole is an important alternative to imprisonment.

Another policy area that needs changing is related to the mandatory sentencing laws that have become popular at the federal and state levels. The "Three Strikes and You're Out" laws and the Rockefeller drug laws have tied the hands of judges, removing their ability to weigh the seriousness of the offense or extenuating circumstances in the sentencing of those convicted. In such situations, judges have no power to assign alternative sentencing, even if they believe it appropriate.

William N. Brownsberger, an assistant attorney general and principal investigator for a study of 1,175 inmates in the Massachusetts prison system, concluded that mandatory sentencing laws are wasting prison resources on nonviolent, low-level offenders The *New York Times* report on the study states that "when researchers looked closely at the records of 151 inmates, nearly half had never been charged with a violent crime in Massachusetts, only one-third had been convicted of a violent crime and only 1 in 12 had been convicted of a serious violent crime like assault with intent to kill." Mandatory drug sentences have caused prison overcrowding and in some cases resulted in sentences more severe than for those convicted of manslaughter. The article goes on to report that "a panel of judges, prosecutors and other criminal justice experts has recommended that judges be allowed to depart from mandatory sentences when a defendant does not have a serious criminal record."[7]

We must also address the limited funding for drug and alcohol treatment programs, high school and post-secondary education, job training, parenting skills, and reintegration training. All of these programs have proven to lower recidivism and reduce governmental costs overall. The above study suggested that the money spent on mandatory sentencing for persons convicted of low-level drug crimes could be better spent on drug and alcohol rehabilitation programs.

Another area of concern is the absence of the community and the victims in the process of deliberation and sentencing. The models of the Native American sentencing circles, Minnesota's juvenile justice approach, and the New Zealand Juvenile Court system offer some clues for viable inclusion of the broader circle that is involved when a crime occurs. We must find a way to end our adversarial approach to criminal justice and build communication among and care for all of those affected by a crime.

Finally, our society must come to terms with the necessity of appropriate training for criminal justice personnel. Far too many of those who choose a career in criminal justice, especially prison guards, are hired without sufficient regard to their motivation, their capacity for human interaction with the persons whom they guard, or their skills to deal with difficult persons in challenging circumstances. Just as the prisoners need training in alternatives to violence, conflict management, and human interaction, so too do the prison personnel. Training alone is not the answer since, in a very profound way, the guards are themselves imprisoned, and the inhumanity of the prison system inevitably takes its toll on them, often leading them to inhumane treatment of the inmates. This is another reason that the entire system must be transformed.

7. *New York Times*, Nov. 25, 1997.

Such policy changes will take enormous effort and patient endurance. They will need to be initiated on both the state and federal levels. They will not happen overnight or all at once. Change will be piecemeal, and since so much depends upon the legislative process, it will inevitably involve compromise and excruciatingly slow progress. Churches and individuals must become involved in the legislative process through lobbying, education of the public, and support for legislators who sponsor restorative measures. Massive letter-writing campaigns, demonstrations, visits to legislative offices, and engagement with and use of the media will all be necessary.

Our nation has been changed before by similar concerted action led by people with a vision of something better. The fight for the abolition of slavery, for women's suffrage, for civil rights, for the end of the Vietnam War all involved public action that changed public policies, laws, and practices. Churches were integrally involved in each of these transformations. We can take courage and gain hope from the victories that have been won.

As long as crime abounds, it is inevitable that most people will be dominated by fear, which will make it difficult to mobilize for changes in the criminal justice system. The greater the fear, the more repressive will be the response. If justice is to have a chance, we must address the roots of crime.

Public Policy and Economic Conversion

The bottom line when it comes to crime is the economic bottom line. As I have mentioned several times, seventy-five percent of all male prisoners in the state of New York come from seven neighborhoods in New York City. These are poverty-ridden, disproportionately crime-generative areas. While it is possible to identify many factors that contribute to criminal behavior — the pervasiveness of drugs, the disintegration of families, the absence of community services, and others — the underlying cause is economic. These communities are desperately poor, not because of drugs, the breakdown of the family, low literacy or poor health; rather, the reverse is true: These conditions are the tragically predictable results of poverty. The unemployment rate among black men ages 18-30 in New York City is higher than fifty percent. The working poor — those working full-time but earning below the poverty line — constitute another enormous proportion of the residents of these neighborhoods. It is next to impossible to build solid family structure, community pride, personal self-esteem, motivation to excel, and civic responsibility when the means for sustaining life at even a subsistence level are not available. In the face of such poverty, drugs become either an escape or a means to income. In the face of despair, the exercise of personal power, including the use of guns, becomes especially heady. In the absence of healthy family life and strong community, gangs become surrogate families.

This is not to revert to an economic determinism; life is simply too complex to reduce all matters to economics. On the other hand, it is impossible to respond responsibly to the issues of crime and justice without addressing our economic system. That so many do not succumb to a life of crime under these overwhelmingly negative odds is a remarkable testimony to the human spirit, to the power of the families that persevere, to the institutions that do not flee, and to the courage of those who resist the temptation to give up. However, despite the miraculous capacity of some people to build out of the ashes, far too many do not.

There are several levels at which conversion of the economic system needs to occur. The first is at the "micro" level, at the grass roots. Until we find ways to rebuild the economies of local neighborhoods so that all have basic needs met, neighborhood beauty is restored, people have the opportunity for satisfying work at a living wage, and decent housing is available, we will continue to encounter despair, rage, and crime. It is as predictable as the rising and setting of the sun.

There are many successful models for the restoration of neighborhoods. One of the oldest ones in New York is the Brooklyn Ecumenical Council. This coalition of thirty-five churches has provided job training, assisted small business development, and begun its own bank. Harlem Interfaith Initiatives has been heavily involved in housing, economic development, education and other means of community empowerment. The Nehemiah Project in East New York has been developing affordable housing that has provided jobs as well as places to live, resulting in the revival of entire sections of the community.

These seven neighborhoods and those like them do not need more McDonald's; they need an infusion of capital, small business development, improved schools, affordable housing, and public works projects such as museums and theaters that provide construction, maintenance, and ongoing professional-level jobs. Large corporations should be encouraged to take advantage of the large tracts of vacant land and buildings in these neighborhoods and to reinvest where industries once thrived. The money for such investment is available. Municipalities throughout the country vie with one another to bring in key businesses by providing tax breaks, low-interest loans, and subsidized rents. Most of these incentives go to keep business in wealthier districts far away from the neighborhoods that need them most. If government can find the money for investments and incentives for pockets of privilege, why can't it do so for impoverished communities? What we fail to see when we refuse to make similar levels of investment in needy neighborhoods is that the costs of impoverishment are borne by the entire society. We need to invest that kind of governmental money in incentives to bring jobs to these neighborhoods. The money saved in lower crime will more than pay for the investment.

However, these investments, whether private or public, must not be provided within the constraints and logic of the market economy. Investors must not come in paying low wages, offering little or no job security, limited benefits, and transferring the profits outside the community, as they have often done in Third World countries. It is imperative that workers be paid living wages and afforded the opportunity for collective bargaining. Profits must be reinvested within the communities in such things as continuing education, job training, family support, childcare, development of the infrastructure, and aesthetic improvements. It is essential that a vital and healthy culture be rebuilt, under the control of the community itself, if poverty and crime are to be effectively challenged. Unless we do this, we guarantee the creation of the next generation of persons caught up in the web of crime.

Attempts to address the economic roots of crime face some major problems. Generally, they are not radical enough. This is a field totally controlled by the market economy. Accordingly, economic development that distributes wealth more fairly, returns the bulk of it to the community in which it is created, and gives serious voice and control to workers and their communities flies in the face of the dominant economic logic. Only a few in the private sector will have the vision or courage to buck the prevailing logic and make such a commitment. Such actions by the private sector will be limited to a few persons and organizations, while the majority stampede elsewhere in search of a better bottom line. This scenario assumes enlightened self-interest, of which we are in short supply.

Nevertheless, there are some businesses, leaders, and investors who do see the bigger picture. The manufacturers of Sweet and Low have rejected the options of mechanizing production or moving from Brooklyn to a less expensive location, and have consciously committed to earn less profit for the sake of the overall benefit of their workers and community. Our churches, synagogues, and mosques should support and encourage persons and companies that make such commitments. They need our support, lest they be seduced by the prevailing culture.

Under the guise of "less government," politicians from both major parties steadily have been reducing their commitment to government investment for the sake of community change and empowerment. Tax breaks have gone to the wealthy while government supports, programs, and even regulatory controls protecting the poor have been evaporating. It is critical that we find ways to challenge our political leaders and support those courageous voices that go against the grain of "less government."

Another source of investment is the wealth of the churches, synagogues, and mosques themselves. A significant number of religious organizations have substantial income and endowments, and could use their wealth to invest in community development and seek a far lower rate of return than that sought by corporations and private individuals. Of course this involves risk, but what is our faith about if not taking risks? Why do congregations need to be afraid of risk when they have millions of dollars in endowments while so many live on the edge of survival?

The second level requiring economic conversion is macroeconomics. Our world is currently dominated by a market economy that places profits before people, economic rights before human rights, and wealth before wholeness. The fundamental assumption that people are entitled to whatever return they can get on their investments, no matter what the cost to others, faces fewer challenges every year.

This book is not essentially about economics, but we cannot avoid the fact that economics is essential. Until we create an economic system that is informed more by the Gospel mandate to care for the least than by the untrammeled right to make all that anyone can, we are doomed to crime and retribution. While there will never be a perfect economic system, our current form of capitalism offers no hope for the end of the cycle of poverty, crime, and punishment. Sweden, with its modified democratic socialism, offers some hope that national wealth creation and a more equitable sharing of that wealth can result in a healthier society, less crime, and a restorative approach. Perhaps it offers us a prototype from which we can seek to develop a truly indigenous response. The shape this could take in the United States remains to be envisioned, but we dare not ignore this task if we are to become a healthy nation. The conversion of our economic system is a fundamental priority for all communities of faith that care about the human condition. We must recognize the economic roots of crime and understand that the fundamental, God-given purpose of wealth is for the health of the whole society. Our faith and common sense teach us that we must find a better way.

The problem with any suggestion of fundamental economic

change as a way of addressing crime and our punitive response to it is that such a suggestion assumes that people are concerned about the consequences of our punitive culture and are willing to seek alternatives. Unfortunately, too often this is not the case. Most seem uninterested in addressing the roots of crime. Far too many don't want healing. They'd rather get even. So we are back where we began — with the spirit of punishment.

A New Spirit: Cultural Conversion

Perhaps the greatest evangelistic task facing the churches today is a conversion from the spirit of punishment to the spirit of healing. A battle is raging for the soul of our nation, a battle that the spirit of punishment appears to be winning. The spirit of punishment will eventually destroy all in its path, including those who do the punishing. It will destroy the soul of our nation. We cannot continue to turn our backs on those who are thirsty or hungry; we cannot continue to lock up those who are oppressed, to ignore the sick, and to close our doors to the stranger, or the heart of our nation will shrivel and die of atrophy.

The church is called to stand on the watchtower, to peer out and see what is coming and to proclaim the truth so that all may hear. God is longing to breathe a new spirit within us as a nation. The breath of our life is fast fading. If we continue in this spirit of punishment, we will eventually become a totally caged society: some living behind the bars of prisons, others behind the bars of privilege. It is already like that for many. The home, business, auto and personal security industries are bullish. More gated communities are being built every month. Finally there will come a time when we have nowhere to go outside our safely barred and policed confines. The end of our mad race to punish is predictable: We too will be prisoners of our own retributive culture.

The church is called upon to share the good news of another way. The Gospel invites us to care for the sick, the harmed, and the criminals — to embrace the lost, accept the prodigal, bind up the stricken. The good news is that no one is beyond the pale of God's love; no one is beyond redemption; no one is outside our family. All are graced. We are all one and we must resist all attempts to divide us into "us" and "them," upright citizens and bestial criminals.

Such transformation requires a radical cultural shift. It involves nothing less than the conversion of the culture itself. Just as there are steps that lead a community or a society inevitably toward bigotry, violence, racism, misogyny, homophobia, and other forms of evil, so too there are steps that move us toward inclusion, justice, and healing. We must proclaim the good news of God's love for all, of the gift of God's grace in all, of the kinship of all, of our interdependence, and of the empowerment of God's spirit in the midst of death and destruction. We have the opportunity to point out the concrete steps that will turn us from retribution to restoration. This will mean preaching from our pulpits that each person bears God's image, that to love another is to love God, that God is a God of love and not of vengeance, that God turns no prodigal away. This cannot be simply generic love or generic acceptance, but must be understood concretely in the life of our society. God loves those who have been convicted of crimes — even murder. God does not simply embrace; God embraces those whom so many have labeled as garbage.

This cultural transformation needs to go far beyond the walls of the churches. We will need to challenge the glorification of retributive violence that is so much a part of our media. We will need to reject every public representation that portrays some people as inferior. We will need to attend to the education of our youth, both in church school and in the public and private schools, so that they understand root causes of criminal activity. We will need to help people move across the artificial boundaries that so long have separated us. We will need to challenge our news media to be more responsible in reporting the whole of the news, not simply what is salacious. The conversion of the soul of our nation will demand a cultural shift at every level. No arena of life can be left untouched.

This is what the various historic images and experiments in theocracy correctly understood. The Gospel addresses every dimension of life, both personal and corporate. It aims at nothing less than a new heaven and a new earth. Where the theocrats and crusaders have been wrong is in thinking that the churches are called upon to direct and govern the culture. The conversion envisioned cannot and dare not be controlled by the churches. The churches are part of the culture, subject to the same punitive spirit and in need of the same conversion. Nevertheless, as churches begin to claim a broader vision of the human community, they have the opportunity to live out the ideal of transformation and to stand in solidarity with all others who have glimpsed something of a restored world. This grants churches neither an exclusive nor even necessarily a primary role. We are called upon to engage in the struggle humbly, yet boldly, with all of the contradictions that inevitably arise.

One last note. To resist the spirit of punishment is not to be soft on crime. It is to be passionately committed to the redemption of all persons and of the society, to justice that is restorative. It does not mean that we should not "get tough," not prevent people from doing acts that harm. It does not mean that we should never put anyone in prison. What it does mean is that in our toughness, in our justice, in our dealing with crime, we should recognize that we are dealing with our brothers and sisters — God's children — and they can come home if we are open to them. Whether they come home is finally their decision, but it can be their decision only if we are ready to receive them with open arms, only if our justice system is a place of restoration. We have no other choice if we wish to survive with dignity as a nation.

INDEX

| | |